AMAZING Bible RACE ™

Wisdom

Job— Solomon

Leg 3

Cover Design: Keely Moore

Contents

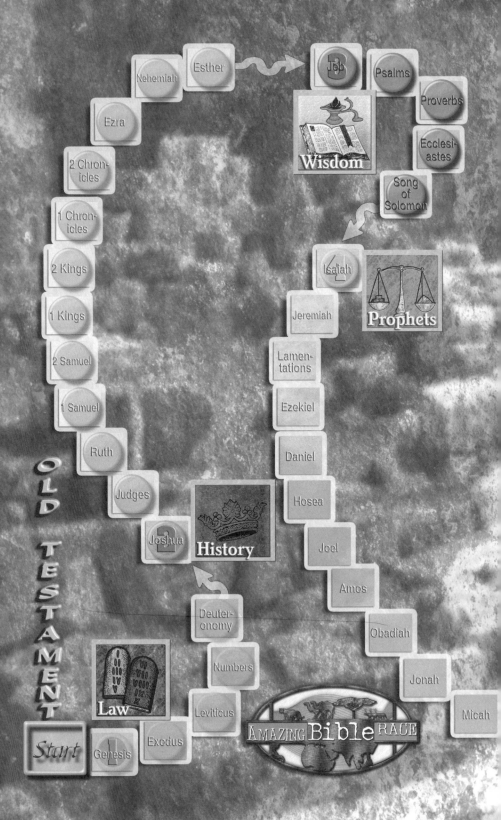

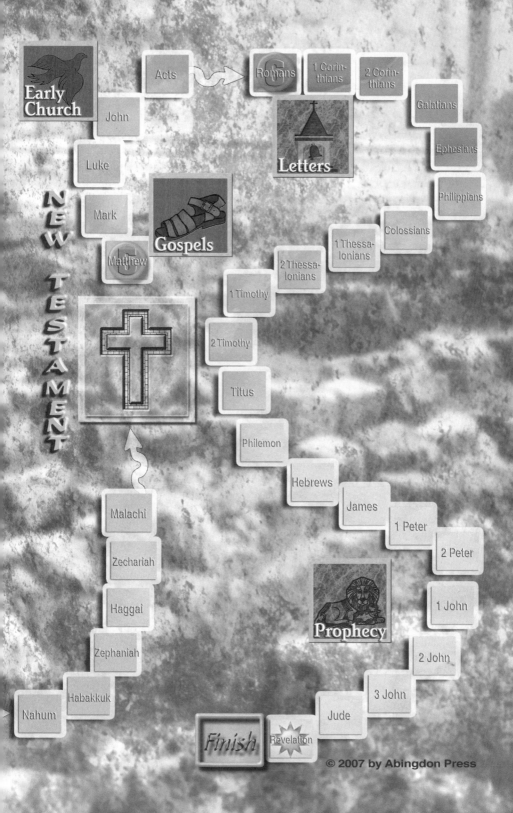

Early Church

Acts

Romans

1 Corin-
thians

2 Corin-
thians

Galatians

John

Ephesians

Luke

Letters

Philippians

Mark

Gospels

Colossians

Matthew

1 Thessa-
lonians

NEW TESTAMENT

2 Thessa-
lonians

1 Timothy

2 Timothy

Titus

Philemon

Hebrews

James

1 Peter

2 Peter

Malachi

Zechariah

1 John

Haggai

Prophecy

Zephaniah

2 John

Habakkuk

3 John

Nahum

Jude

Finish

Revelation

© 2007 by Abingdon Press

Moving On

Get ready for an emotional ride through the Scriptures during Leg 3 of the Amazing Bible Race. The Wisdom literature ahead of you presents some tough terrain for traveling. You will hear the agonies of heartfelt cries, as humans suffer and question God. You will ask the hard questions about the meaning of life. Unfortunately, you may not always get the answers you anticipate nor ones that satisfy completely. You will experience the heights of joy and the exhilaration of romantic love.

As you run this Leg, keep a few things in mind:

1. **Be a team player**—You and your teammates can work together to get through difficult passages and hurdles. So ask for help if you need it, and be quick to offer your help to your teammates as well. Encourage your teammates to stay focused on the Race. Working together makes this an even greater experience.

2. **Give it your all**—Devote yourself to the goal before you. You are accomplishing a major feat, with excellent progress so far. Don't give up now. Keep digging through the Scriptures to learn more of who God is and who you are. Now isn't the time to take shortcuts or to give up.

3. **Focus on the journey, not on the prize**—The points and the competition are a lot of fun; and of course, you should set out to do your best. But the most important aspect of the Race is the grand prize you receive as you study the Word and meet God in Scripture daily. Don't get lost in the competition and miss the deeper blessing of God's changing you from the inside out.

4. **Use a Bible translation that you understand**—You may choose to listen to the Scripture on the Internet, CD, your MP3 player, or your smart phone. Maybe you need to use a contemporary version of the Bible, such as the *Contemporary English Version* or *Today's New International Version,* which uses everyday common words and sentence structures. More scholarly translations include the *New Revised Standard Version* or the *New International Version.* For a particularly confusing passage, try reading a paraphrase in *The Message.* You can read from these Bibles and many others online at websites such as *bible.crosswalk.com* or *www.biblegateway.com.* Read what you understand so that you can understand what you read.

AMAZING Bible RACE

The Rules

Rule 1
Follow steps 1–4 for each daily reading.

Rule 2
As a team, answer the Weekly Challenges and submit them to the website.

Rule 3
Accomplish any Fast Forwards that appear in your Runner's Reader. A Fast Forward appears periodically and is a life-application exercise for your team. You'll be asked to find a way to apply the Bible reading to your life. For example, if you're reading about feeding the hungry, you might decide to serve food at a local rescue mission. To receive credit for the outing, you must have someone make a video of it or take a photo of your group in action; then upload it to *amazingbiblerace.com*.

Rule 4
Help your teammates overcome any Hurdles. When you face a particularly difficult section of Scripture or feel that you're getting stuck, you might see a Hurdle. Hurdles allow you to skim that particular Scripture passage and accomplish or perform a task based on the Bible lesson or solve a quiz on *amazingbiblerace.com* to "quiz-out" of that section.

Rule 5
Earn as many points as possible for your team. You gain points by finishing your daily readings, solving Weekly Challenges, participating in the Fast Forwards, solving the extra quizzes, or looking on the map and taking a quiz. The more effort you put in to the Race, the more you'll get out of it—and the more points you'll receive!

Rule 6
The adult mentor is the team coach who keeps team members encouraged and motivated. The coach should check in at least once a week to make sure that everyone is reading and that you have a time scheduled to work together (by IM, e-mail, text message, or phone conversation) to solve the Weekly Challenge.

Rule 7
Support your team and work together.

Rule 8
Have fun!

Once Upon a Time...
Job 1–2

1 Scouting the Terrain

You've probably heard the expression, "the patience of Job." But do you know the story upon which it's based?

Today you'll begin reading the Bible's wisdom literature, starting with the Book of Job. The author of Job is unknown but is regarded to have been an Israelite poet. The book reads like a folk tale. It's the story of a righteous man who suffers as a result of a competition between God and Satan. He refuses to curse God and is eventually restored to greater blessings.

Job's story can be a bit confusing because it doesn't fit nicely into a traditional Bible story outline. You won't find a theme of "you reap what you sow" here. It also destroys the notion of fair rewards and punishment based on one's actions. Job is a righteous man and has done no wrong, yet he suffers unimaginably.

Scholars disagree as to the treatment of righteous suffering in the book. Some believe that the Book of Job refuses to answer why God's people suffer, while others see Job's experience as a testing of his faith (orchestrated by the hand of God) for God's glory that was designed to bring Job closer to God.

- Before you read the text, answer this question: How do you explain suffering in your own life? What are your thoughts about God's role in human suffering?

Trailblazers

- **God**
- **Satan**
- **Job**
- **Job's wife**
- **Eliphaz**
- **Bildad**
- **Zophar**

Road Signs

- **"sheep ... camels ... oxen ... donkeys"** (1:3): Wealth was measured by the amount of livestock one possessed.
- **loathsome sores** (2:7): What type of sores Job had is uncertain.
- **potsherd** (2:8): This is a piece of broken pottery, a shard.
- **seven days and seven nights** (2:13): The three friends' behavior displays the most intense grief. Cultural protocol dictated that Job should be the first to speak.

2 NOW READ JOB 1–2.

3 Switchback

In the opening chapters of Job, we see action in two locations: heaven and earth.

Job is described as blameless and upright. These descriptions do not mean that he was sinless but that he loved and was devoted to God. We see that Job is blessed in all ways: with wealth, with family, and with health.

Then, one day, Job's life is turned upside down. All is lost. Not only is he emotionally miserable from losing everyone and everything he holds dear, he is also physically miserable from having sores all over his body. What Job doesn't know is that God has permitted Satan to attack Job, his possessions, and his family.

Job's response to his trials comes as the rest of the book unfolds. Satan questioned Job's motives for his devotion to God. Satan also claimed that Job would curse God once his suffering was intensified. Job, however, proves that Satan is, indeed, a liar. He continues to praise God even in the midst of sorrow and pain.

• How would you answer someone who cites this story as proof that God is not good and does not care about human suffering?

 Satan appears as the accuser in another courtroom scene (similar to the one in Job 1:6-12). Find the reference in the Book of Zechariah, then take a quiz at *amazingbiblerace.com* to show what you have learned.

4 Prayer

God, thank you for being with me through the good times and the bad times. Amen.

I Wish I'd Never Been Born!
Job 3–4

1 Scouting the Terrain

Job 2 ends with a heavy silence. Cultural protocol dictated that Job be the first to speak. And when he does open his mouth, he does so with fierce emotion. Although Satan believes that Job will curse God—and Job's wife advises him to do so—he does not. He comes really close, though. He doesn't curse God explicitly, but he does question God's wisdom in giving him life. Job curses the day he was born, asking why he wasn't stillborn or why he is still living.

Eliphaz is the first friend to speak. In this opening speech, Eliphaz begins politely, asking permission to speak and complimenting Job's teaching. Eliphaz quickly moves to using words of accusation, pointing out Job's impatience. He reminds Job to take comfort in his righteousness and trust in God's justice. Maybe Eliphaz is saying this for his own benefit, rather than Job's. He knows Job's reputation and cannot understand why such suffering has come upon his friend. What must Job have done to deserve this?

Trailblazers

• **Job**
• **Eliphaz**

• Have you ever been so depressed that you asked God why you were even born? What helped you through that tough time of questioning?

2 NOW READ JOB 3–4.

10

③ Switchback

Well, this is it. You've reached the nitty-gritty: the hard questions; the hard passages; the hard concepts to grasp about God, humanity, suffering, evil, and love. Bible scholars have long debated why bad things happen to good people. They cannot agree on one answer.

From a human perspective, we believe that it makes sense to assume that bad things happen to only people who do evil. We see that as fair, right?

But look again at the life of Job. He is upright and blameless. He has not done the type of evil that would call for this type of suffering. Likewise, we know many modern-day examples of persons suffering greatly, such as children dying from disease or lack of proper nutrition and health care. It all leaves us wondering, "What did they do to deserve that?"

Pray that the Holy Spirit would give you the proper perspective of suffering and justice as you pour over Job's story.

• Why do bad things happen to good people?

It's book report time! Suffering is part of the fabric of the history of the church. With your team, find a book about a true story of Christian suffering. (If you need some suggested titles, check the list at *amazingbiblerace.com*). Your race director must approve your book selection, and each member of the team must read the book. Schedule a time to present your book report. Your report can be as creative as you choose, and it may resemble a book club discussion. Talk about your perspectives on human suffering, evil, justice, and God's love and point out any changes in those perspectives from having read the book. Be sure to note any references the book makes to Job's experience. Upload a video of your team's presentation at *amazingbiblerace.com* for points.

④ Prayer

Lord, be with me during times of suffering. Amen.

You Can't Put God in a Box
Job 5–6

WEEK
1
◆
DAY
3

1 Scouting the Terrain

Trailblazers
- **Job**
- **Eliphaz**

Eliphaz continues his argument, chastising Job's previous outburst. He outlines again the eventual outcome for the foolish: ruin and hardship. He tries to employ the "you reap what you sow" philosophy in 5:6, claiming that Job must have brought all of this trouble on himself. His life is rotten, so he must have done something equally rotten to be going through this now.

You can almost hear Eliphaz taking an arrogant posture, clearing his throat, and straightening his shirt in verse 8. "Well, Job, if I were you . . ." He tells Job that he should seek God and commit his cause to God. Eliphaz follows with praises for God with a cut-and-dried illustration of God's justice in the world. Yep, Eliphaz has it all figured out. He needs for the world to work the way he has described it. When it does, his God fits in his tidy box. The problem is this: God is way too big for a box, and Job's experience flies in the face of everything Eliphaz has just said.

- When have you made assumptions about God just to explain away something to your own satisfaction?

2 NOW READ JOB 5–6.

3 Switchback

Toward the end of Job 6, Job calls into question his friends' faithfulness. After hearing Eliphaz's speech, Job is quick to point out that his friend's words are not comforting. He accuses Eliphaz and the others of being fair-weather friends. The minute Job's circumstances go sour, the friends withdraw their compassion.

Our culture is obsessed with winning outcomes. Compassionate loyalty is hard to come by. You've probably experienced the wavering devotion of sports fans. When the town's team is winning, the people are supportive. When the team has a losing record, everybody is quick to offer critical advice for the coaches.

Suffering, poverty, hunger, disease—even losing—are all part of life, though. The degrees to which one experiences these things may vary, but these experiences will come. We all can't be on top all of the time. We all can't win all of the time. Jesus never promised us an easy ride. In fact, he promised the opposite (see John 16:33).

Do your friends safely trust in you? Are you devoted and loyal? Will you offer comfort to others who are experiencing trial? Think of persons who are hurting who have no advocates. How will you reach out to them in love, without judgment?

• Do you have an Eliphaz in your life? Have you been an Eliphaz to a hurting friend? Describe the situation(s) below.

4 Prayer

God, help me be a good friend to those who suffer. Amen.

Screams of Agony
Job 7–10

1 Scouting the Terrain

Job continues to protest that he is innocent. He says that life is very short, so he's going to make his complaint known. His life is over, he says; so he might as well get it out. Job confronts God with what has become of his life. Job is full of questions, wondering why he is the object of divine attention.

Trailblazers
- **Job**
- **Bildad**

Bildad, the second of Job's friends, speaks. Bildad isn't any more comforting than Eliphaz was. Bildad, like Eliphaz, wants to reassure himself of God's justice. He arrives at the same conclusion: The proof of Job's guilt is that he is experiencing such tragedy.

Job responds with continued questioning, addressing God. By the end of chapter 10, Job's rant becomes almost paranoid, accusing God of hunting Job as a wild beast stalks its prey (verse 16).

• When have you questioned God's actions in your life?

• When have you felt that God "had it in for you"? Is feeling that way right or wrong? Why?

2 NOW READ JOB 7–10.

3 Switchback

When life is sweet, it's easy to praise God. It's easy to have faith and trust in God's good plans.

When the going gets tough, however, the tough—well, the tough falter and wilt. Tough times try us, tempt us, and tear us down. Some people actually abandon their faith while going through a crisis. The harsh circumstances of life overwhelm them, and they believe that they can find no relief in God.

Job moves to the edge of abandoning his faith but never quite goes overboard. Some may consider Job as the Bible's most tragic (and ultimately, most triumphant) figure (aside from Christ). He has it all. He loses it all and suffers to the point of near death. He never curses God, though; and his faith gives him hope for redemption. In the end, Job's suffering ends; and he is more greatly blessed than before.

• Does suffering bring you closer to God or farther from God?

• How is Job's experience tragic and triumphant?

4 Prayer

God, when suffering comes, strengthen my faith. Amen.

Just Get Over It
Job 11–14

Scouting the Terrain

The third of Job's friends, Zophar, speaks. He's the harshest of the group. Zophar is quick to point out that Job's claims of innocence are just babbling. Zophar tells Job to give it a rest. He says that Job getting off easy. God should be harder on Job.

Trailblazers
• Zophar
• Job

Zophar reminds Job that no human can fully understand the ways of God. God is omniscient; God has infinite awareness, understanding, and insight. Therefore, punishment is unavoidable and beyond human comprehension. "Get over it, Job," Zophar seems to say. So Zophar is another friend who believes the worst about Job.

Zophar has answers, though. Zophar tells Job to turn from his sin and return to God. Zophar promises Job an end to his suffering as well as rewards that will come when he repents: security, hope, light, and prosperity. But Job is not buying it.

Today's reading continues with Job's chastising his friends and pleading with God. Job persists in believing that God is just, and he asks God to explain this to him. Job laments again the brevity and sufferings of life and wishes that it would all just end.

• Have you ever found the circumstances of life to be at odds with what you thought you understood? What did you do? How did you reconcile what you believed with what was happening? Did the circumstance change what you believed? Why, or why not?

2 NOW READ
JOB 11–14.

3 Switchback

Zophar is so full of himself. Smug and arrogant, he's got a word or two for Job. He's full of criticism, assumptions, and baseless predictions. He's a really horrible advisor.

Do you ever stop to examine all the messages that bombard you daily? We have so much talking to us, singing to us, and displaying words to us. So much information vies for our attention. How do you sort through it? How do you determine a message's credibility? How do you pick out the Zophars in your own life?

The Word of God should be your standard measure for messages about belief and action. Beyond that, you should have safe advisors upon which you can lean. Your parents and other adults rooted in the faith should be among the first to whom you turn when you have questions. Close, devoted Christian friends should also be allowed into your inner circle.

When you insulate your heart and your mind with these safeguards, discerning all the competing messages, faulty assumptions, and downright lies becomes easier. You need as much ammunition as possible so that you are equipped to tune out the Zophars in your life.

• What is one difficult situation with which you are currently struggling? Who among your safe, inner circle will you trust to help you?

Water Break

You're doing a great job making your way through the Book of Job. It can be confusing and repetitive—maybe even a little bit depressing at times. Keep going, though. Congratulations on the progress you've already made.

4 Prayer

God, ground my decision-making in the truth of your Word. Amen.

With Friends Like These . . .
Job 15–17

1 Scouting the Terrain

The second cycle of speeches begins with each friend speaking and Job responding in turn. Here Eliphaz ups the ante. Eliphaz and the others defend their theology against Job, who seems to be a blasphemer. Eliphaz speaks about the fate of the wicked, using metaphors to say that the wicked, not the righteous, suffer. He implies, therefore, that Job must be a wicked man, as evidenced by his suffering. Job replies that their speeches are of no comfort to him and that they would see things differently if they were in his shoes.

Trailblazers
• Job
• Eliphaz

In chapters 16 and 17, Job describes at length how God has afflicted him and pours out his sorrow and grief. Much of the imagery Job uses compares God's actions to those of a criminal.

• Do you think that Job is angry with God? Why, or why not?

• Describe a time when you poured out your heart to God in sorrow, grief, or anger.

• How have you reacted when one your deeply held beliefs was challenged by someone else?

2 NOW READ JOB 15–17.

3 Switchback

When have you been angry, really fuming angry? Anger is a powerful emotion that can cause us to sin or that can motivate us to good works. The Bible speaks of the Lord's anger about the people's abandonment of the covenant (Deuteronomy 29:21-29) and Christ's anger with the corrupt elite who exploit the poor by charging admission for worship in the Temple (Matthew 21:12-17). Job 28:28 reminds us that, although our anger sometimes leads us to lash out at God, we must continually balance our complaints with humility and reverence toward God. Humans will always fall short of understanding the ways of God, so we will undoubtedly be lead to angry questioning. We can be reassured that our emotions are not new to God; and when handled with a healthy respect, our emotions can lead us closer to God.

• When you think about times when you have been angry, how would considering the anger of God, Jesus, Job, and other biblical figures affect you?

• Is being angry with God ever justified? Should someone repent of being angry with God? How, do you think, does God view our anger with others? with ourselves? with God?

• How can you balance your heart's honest cries of anguish to God with a reverence for your Creator?

Road Signs

• **Sackcloth** (16:15): During Bible times, this dark-colored, coarse fabric, probably resembling burlap, was made of goat or camel hair and was used to make grain bags and inexpensive clothing. A garment of sackcloth, usually in the form of a shirt or loin cloth, was so scratchy that it was worn as a sort of self-punishment, as a demonstration to God and others of the wearer's extreme remorse, or as a sign of mourning for the loss of a loved one. Some people were so poor that they wore only sackcloth clothing.

4 Prayer

Lord, help me in my anger to not sin and to always regard you with reverence. Amen.

Thanks, but no Thanks
Job 18–21

① Scouting the Terrain

Bildad rebukes Job and tells him to be reasonable. He says that Job knows what is true and that he just needs to accept it. Job asks how long they will keep "tormenting [him] with words." Isn't he already miserable enough? Job says clearly for the first time, "God has wronged me" (19:6) and appeals to his friends for sympathy and understanding. Zophar says that Job's accusations against God disturb him. Zophar, like Eliphaz and Bildad before him, asserts that the theology of divine retribution, or payback, for transgressions is true and that Job needs to accept that he has done something wrong. Job answers that he is complaining to God, not to his friends. He argues against their ideas by saying that wicked men often have happy and fulfilling lives, disproving his friends' abstract claims about the fate of the wicked.

Trailblazers
- Job
- Bildad
- Zophar

- When have you withheld sympathy for a friend because you thought that he or she deserved his or her suffering? When have you said or wanted to say, "I told you so"?

- Would you speak to one of your friends the way Eliphaz, Bildad, and Zophar did? If you wouldn't, what would you do instead?

② NOW READ JOB 18–21.

3 Switchback

While his friends keep insisting that their theology is correct, Job disagrees. Despite his anger with God, Job's hope is in the ultimate goodness of God. This deep devotion that defied his uncomfortable situation and his misinformed advisors is a sign of Job's true identity as a righteous man.

• Describe a time when your circumstances made your beliefs about God difficult. How did you use the truth of Scripture to uphold your beliefs? How did Scripture challenge your beliefs?

Road Signs

• "Escaped by the skin of my teeth" (19:20b): This idiom, apparently first used by Job, has come to mean "hardly, barely, with difficulty."

• What do you find comforting in your most difficult times? Is this something that honors God?

fast forward On Day 5, you'll read about the role of remembrance in Job's perseverance through his suffering. What are ways that you worship God through the role of remembrance? With your team, organize and lead a worship service for your large group or for a younger Sunday school class. Each element of the service should incorporate an element of remembering the good things God has done in your lives. Blog about or videotape the worship service, then upload it to *amazingbiblerace.com* for points.

4 Prayer

God, help me see past my own narrow understanding and see the world the way you see it. Help me reflect your compassion to all those who need it. Amen.

21

Nonexistent Secret Sin
Job 22–24

Scouting the Terrain

The third cycle of speeches begins, although it does not take quite the same form as the first two cycles. Zophar does not speak this time, and Bildad's speech is extremely brief. Job's speeches also take on a decidedly different tone. Eliphaz accuses Job of social injustices that caused homelessness and hunger. He seems to be digging into Job's past, trying to come up with an explanation as to why God would impose such suffering. If Job can see his own wickedness, then his suffering may make sense. Job does not directly refute Eliphaz's accusations, although Job maintains that were he to state his case before God, he would not be condemned.

• When have you questioned the reason for suffering in your life or in others' lives?

Trailblazers
• **Job**
• **Eliphaz**
• **Bildad**

• Why do "good" things happen to some "good" people, while other "good" people suffer? Why do some "bad" people seem to prosper?

NOW READ JOB 22–24.

3 Switchback

Some popular Christian teachers today say that people with authentic faith will prosper (financially, physically, emotionally, and so forth), while those with weaker or little faith will suffer. These teachers emphasize material wealth, good health, and overall prosperity as being the indisputable sign of the degree of one's devotion to God. If one is poor or sick, then, these ministers teach that fixing one's relationship with God will make one rich and healthy. Eliphaz's speech echoes these modern-day teachings, while Job rejects Eliphaz's suggestions. Job maintains his innocence and his allegiance to and hope in God. Scripture reassures us of Job's righteousness (review Job 1), so Eliphaz's speech is seriously off base.

• Who is to blame for human suffering such as poverty, hunger, homelessness, and sickness?

• How would you respond to a friend or church leader who accuses you of atrocious, unrepentant, and habitual sin as a reason for suffering in your life, such as a fatal illness?

• Have you ever understood there to be a connection between sin and suffering? If yes, describe it here and discuss it with your team members.

4 Prayer

Lord, please help me see past my day-to-day circumstances, having faith in you even when it feels like you're absent. Amen.

Our Great God
Job 25–28

① Scouting the Terrain

Bildad gives a short speech contrasting the greatness of God with the worthlessness of humanity. It's another round of misinformed advice for Job. Even in its sin, humanity retains its image of God, which gives dignity and value to each person. Job comes back with a long speech about God's infinity and all-seeing eye. Job implies that our knowledge is finite, but he maintains that humanity has only to trust that God is in control. We will never understand God's ways fully. Job sums it up by saying, "Fear-of-the-Lord—that's Wisdom" (28:28, *Message*). True wisdom has a trusting respect for and awe of God.

Trailblazers
• Bildad
• Job

• How do you feel about not understanding all the ways of God?

• If we can't fully understand the way God works, why should we even try?

② NOW READ JOB 25–28.

3 Switchback

These chapters again bring us to the contrast of finite humanity with an infinite God. Job's speech expresses the idea that wisdom (here meaning full knowledge of God and the universe) is hidden from us. We can never fully understand God. We can know and understand only in part. We may have a piece of the puzzle, but we should not confuse grasping our little piece with the ability to see the whole picture.

• Is it possible to talk about our understanding of God and still recognize that we don't have it all figured out? How does one do this?

• What does the recognition of God's infinite nature contribute to our discussion of why "bad" things happen to "good" people and "good" things happen to "bad" people?

Road Signs

• **Abaddon** (uh-BAD-uhn) (26:6; 28:22): In Hebrew, this word literally means "destruction." It is also another name for *Sheol,* the Hebrew term for the underworld, and is the dwelling place of the dead.

4 Prayer

God, I know that I can't understand it all. Please help me understand everything I can, and give me the peace to know that you are in control. Amen.

Job's Defense
Job 29–31

WEEK

2

◇

DAY

5

① Scouting the Terrain

This is Job's final speech, ending the three cycles. He longs for the past when he enjoyed God's blessing and favor. Now, Job feels abandoned. He feels all have turned against him. Not even his friends

Trailblazer

• Job

will believe that he didn't do anything to deserve this. Job swears his innocence, still wanting to believe that bad things only happen to the wicked. He still hopes for a resolution that complies with his ideas of God's justice. In Chapter 30, Job names how each blessing has been taken from him. He cries out to God in anguish and despair. Job defends himself, declaring his innocence of horrid moral sin.

• How do the peaks of the Christian walk (the "mountain top," so to speak, when God's blessing and favor is abundantly clear in your life) help you through the darker times, the valleys of suffering and despair?

• What advice would you give to someone who is going through a dark time of crisis?

② NOW READ JOB 29–31.

③ Switchback

The Bible is full of examples of remembrance. Part of our Christian journey is to be lived remembering. We are to tell the stories of God's goodness to the next generation (Psalm 78:4). Remembrance aids our discipleship because we learn about our God in the past, which is a reliable predictor of God's faithfulness to us in the future. Because God doesn't change, we are assured that our covenant-making, covenant-keeping God will be faithful to keep God's promises to us.

• What remembrances or rituals help you focus on God's faithfulness in the middle of your or someone else's suffering?

• How might you view your current life ten years from now?

Road Signs

• **Mallow** (30:4): Due to its unpleasant nature as a food source, this herb's dry, disk-shaped fruit was used only in desperate times.

 In chapter 31, Job defends himself against the accusation that he is a wicked man getting what he deserves. His speech denies several categories of moral sin. With your team, outline chapter 31, identify these categories, then match them to the appropriate commandment from God's Law. When you're finished, take a quiz at *amazingbiblerace.com* and check your research.

④ Prayer

Lord, when I suffer, help me remember the truths of Scripture. May my memories of your goodness and blessing encourage me. Amen.

Water Break

You're more than halfway finished with Job. Take a break now and get ready to hear from a new Bible figure next week. You're doing great!

27

Voice of Reason?
Job 32–33

1 Scouting the Terrain

Suddenly a new figure, Elihu, speaks. We don't know whether he has been standing by during the whole dialogue between Job and his friends or is a new arrival. Elihu is the only figure in Job with a Hebrew name, so some scholars think that he was a later addition to make the story more Jewish and to give another perspective on the issues being discussed. Elihu rebukes Job for justifying himself rather than justifying God.

Trailblazers

• **Elihu**
• **Job**
• **Eliphaz**
• **Bildad**
• **Zophar**

Scholars disagree as to Elihu's role. Some view him as a messenger between God and Job, who gives Job a reason for his suffering: to bring Job closer to God. Other scholars dismiss Elihu, saying that, while believers will certainly grow closer to God during suffering, a good God could never ordain suffering (and, therefore, associate with an evil source that produces suffering). Trying to find a reason for suffering is pointless; suffering just is. What we do with suffering and how we respond to it should be our focus. (FYI: The fancy term for the theology of suffering is *theodicy*.)

• Is Elihu's answer to suffering more satisfying than the answers of Job and his friends? Why, or why not?

2 NOW READ JOB 32–33.

3 Switchback

Depending on how you view Elihu's message, you may find him arrogant, rude, and full of himself or reasonable, wise, and necessary. Is his speech an interruption or a welcome explanation? Again, scholars disagree on his character, his delivery, and his message. We do know that he is considerably younger than the other men and speaks up to say what's on his mind.

• Regardless of your assessment of Elihu, should his age and/or lack of experience be reason enough for dismissing him or his comments? Why, or why not?

Road Signs

• **"In his own eyes** (32:1)**:** Because Job believes himself to be "righteous in his own eyes," his friends know that they can say nothing that will change Job's mind about his own innocence. Later in the Bible, the same words are used in Proverbs (26:5; 30:12) to describe the attitude of a fool.

Prayer

Lord, I thank you that you have given wisdom to young and old alike. Make me wiser, I pray. Amen.

Worldwide, people suffer materially, financially, nutritionally, emotionally, and spiritually. With your team, research a need and a tangible way you can help. You may choose to help a large organization based overseas or a family in your church or community. Create a written out three-month plan of commitment. Upload the plan or a scan of it to *amazingbiblerace.com* for points. In order to receive full credit, you must also provide photos or videos of team members participating in whatever your team has committed to do.

Choice Words
Job 34–35

Scouting the Terrain

Elihu explains how the men have been asking the wrong question all along. They have been debating whether or not Job is righteous, assuming that God rewards and punishes based on righteousness. Elihu turns the conversation away from Job and to God. Elihu argues for the righteousness of God's character, saying that God is fair and just. He claims that Job's experience is not trustworthy because his propositions contradict those aspects of God that are a matter of accepted tradition. Elihu's reasoning, therefore, implies that our experiences should never be used to question God.

• Where do you turn to learn truths about God?

Trailblazers

• Elihu
• Job
• Eliphaz
• Bildad
• Zophar

• What is the relationship between personal experience and the church's tradition as it relates to your understanding of who God is?

NOW READ
JOB 34–35.

3 Switchback

Job's prayer form may have caught Elihu off-guard. Job cries out to God and uses legal terminology in his prayers. Elihu criticizes Job's prayers, which are different from the "accepted" form. Job's heartfelt pleas challenge the traditional ways to approach God. Worship of God has long been based on traditions handed down through generations. Some of the church's worship traditions are rooted in Scripture, while others originate from a more human source.

• What is worship supposed to look like? Why?

• What worship traditions are celebrated at your church and/or in your denomination? Speak with your worship leader(s) and/or pastor to find out why your worship service is organized the way it is. Discover the meaning behind the elements of the worship service.

• When have you been criticized for a differing belief about the "right" way to worship, sing, or pray?

4 Prayer

Lord, help me to see past my own limited understanding and to appreciate the infinite nature of your wisdom and justice. Amen.

31

Fear of the Lord
Job 36–37

Scouting the Terrain

Elihu's last speech is his reflection on God's character. He is no longer quoting or refuting Job or his friends. This speech seems to step out of the main story for a moment and provide a broader reflection that sets us up for God's appearance in the next chapters. Elihu says that God is greater than any of our understandings. While our ideas about God are on the right track, we must always recognize the finite nature of our knowledge and always be in awe and wonder at the infinite nature of God. Complete understanding of God's ways is unattainable; the truly wise accept this and revere God all the more.

WEEK
3
◆
DAY
3

• Are you comforted or frustrated to think that God is beyond our capacity to fully understand? Why?

Trailblazers

• Elihu
• Job
• Eliphaz
• Bildad
• Zophar

• When you accept that full knowledge of God is not possible in this life, are you overcome with awe and praise? Why, or why not? What would it take to create awe and praise in your heart?

NOW READ
JOB 36–37.

3 Switchback

God is infinite and we are finite, so we can never fully understand God's ways. We are discussing issues of ultimate significance with partial information at best. We have to be humble enough to realize that even the smartest theologian is ultimately out of his or her league when talking about the ways of God. This is Elihu's main point in these speeches, and God's response to all of these conversations (which we will read tomorrow) seems to validate this idea.

• Elihu says that bad weather is a form of God's judgment. How would you explain Hurricane Katrina and other natural disasters in light of these verses?

4 Prayer

Lord, help me always be in wonder and awe of you. Let me never limit you by the smallness of my own understanding. Amen.

When You Get What You Ask for
Job 38–41

1 Scouting the Terrain

And now it's God's turn. The Lord responds to the speeches, shedding some light on all that has been said. Interestingly, God doesn't mention Job's torment nor does God provide an answer to the reason for Job's suffering. Instead, God outlines the act of Creation, implying Job's weakness and God's omnipotence. Job should keep that in mind next time he calls God's character into question. Job replies that he sees how small he is compared to God and withdraws his offer to plead his case before God, since God knows the whole story anyway.

Trailblazer
• God

• What is the significance of God's response to Job? What kind of answer do you suppose Job was expecting?

• How does pondering God's power lead you to worship God? lead you to repentance? Describe how this type of meditation leads you to other thoughts or spiritual habits.

2 NOW READ JOB 38–41.

3 Switchback

We hear about some interesting creatures in God's speech to Job. While these creatures' names conjure images of a sci-fi movie, no one knows exactly what the Behemoth (bi-HEE-muhth) and the Leviathan (li-VIGH-uh-thuhn) are. Scholars have speculated that the Behemoth may have been an elephant or hippopotamus, while the Leviathan may have been a crocodile. Other scholars believe that they were mythical creatures, that Leviathan was a seven-headed sea monster that could glide and coil.

Regardless of their true identity, these creatures serve important roles in God's speech. They are examples of power and pride that Job couldn't overcome. They show that God's powers of creation and re-creation are stronger than the power of the chaotic. In the midst of considering these illustrations, we are reminded that mighty God of Creation became a human and dwelt among us. Christ the Son suffered even more than Job did to show us the extent of God's love for us. That is truly the greatest mystery of faith.

• How does it feel to know that the infinite God cares about the tiniest of finite creatures? What does this say about God's character?

Road Signs

• **"Gird ... your loins"** (38:3): This phrase is a call to action that means "get ready." In the days when men wore robes, they usually wore them free flowing. However, the robes got in the way during vigorous movement—physical labor, fighting, running—or when wading in water while fishing. To gird his loins, a man would pull the hem edge of his robe up between his legs and tuck it into his belt or other tie around his waist. The result might have looked something like pants.

 The divine speech (Job 38–39) features images of nature to convey the creative power of God. With your team, dissect the divine speech, noting which images of nature are named. Then take a quiz to check your work at *amazingbiblerace.com*.

4 Prayer

Lord, help me be humble enough to know just how little I really know. Amen.

Repentance and Restoration
Job 42

Scouting the Terrain

The divine speech from the whirlwind creates real change in Job's heart. He repents immediately—not of living an evil life—but of questioning the goodness of God. Job confesses the Lord's greatness and submits to God's wisdom. God then says that Job has spoken rightly of him, while Job's three friends have not (Elihu is not mentioned). God tells Eliphaz, Bildad, and Zophar to make sacrifices for speaking against God's true nature and restores Job's fortunes with new children, land, and cattle. Job lives out the rest of his life happily, having learned the true nature of God from his experience.

Trailblazers
- God
- Job
- Job
- Eliphaz
- Bildad
- Zophar

• Job seems to have been commended for questioning his ideas about God. Although he was angry for most of the book, Job allowed himself to learn form the experience and so he benefited from it. What does this tell us about how we should treat our ideas about God?

WEEK
3
◆
DAY
5

• Considering Job's experience and God's response, how will you now view God during times of suffering?

2 NOW READ JOB 42.

Switchback

One could take the conclusion of Job to mean that all who suffer will eventually be rewarded. But we see people every day who continue to suffer until the day they die. Job's outcome doesn't guarantee that everyone who suffers righteously will be restored to blessing in this life, but God does guarantee rewards in the new world to come for those who suffer righteously (Romans 8:18-39). If Christians have any basis for hope, it is the hope of ultimate justice and an ultimate end to suffering for all people.

• Reflect on the Book of Job. Why, do you think, do "bad" things happen to "good" people? Why do "good" things happen to "bad" people? How have your answers to these questions changed since you began reading the Book of Job? Discuss your thoughts with your team members and on your blog.

Water Break

Whew! You're finished with Job's suffering! Good job! Job is an incredibly difficult book to understand and apply to modern life, but you did it. Way to go! Don't stop now. Up next: Psalms.

 Prayer

Lord, help me always understand and learn more about the infinite nature of your wisdom and grace. Amen.

And I Will Sing
Psalms 1–10

1 Scouting the Terrain

The word *psalm* means "song," and the Hebrew title for this book is translated "Book of Praises."

Trailblazer
• David

One of the most prolific psalm-writers is David. Almost half of the psalms are credited to him, but at least one was written five hundred years after his birth.

The psalms are written as poetry, as a conversation between God and Israel. Some are public and served as official acts of praise or petition. Others are personal laments from places of pain and hardship. The psalms come from actual worship of God by the community.

God's people have learned from these prayers, prayed these prayers, and adapted these prayers for countless generations. Jesus himself quoted twice from the psalms (22:1 and 31:5). In the psalms, the Church has found comfort knowing that the most faithful persons—even David, the great king—experienced extreme emotion. So join your voice with the voices of the psalmists and God's people as you sing the psalms.

• What is one of your favorite hymns or praise choruses? Why do you like it so much?

• What does it mean to you that a prayer written thousands of years ago can be applicable to you today?

2 NOW READ PSALMS 1–10.

Switchback

The Book of Psalms begins by identifying two types of people: the righteous and the wicked. The righteous follow the ways of God, while the wicked do not. The righteous will prosper and live on while the wicked will fall away. One is either righteous or wicked; no third option is given.

Even the righteous will face times of trial. When things look bleak, David remains faithful to God and knows that God will protect and deliver him. When it seems as though the whole world is against us, we can follow David's model. Throughout the psalms, you will see that even though David cries out in distress, he has unshaking confidence in the goodness of God. David trusts God to hear his prayers and uphold him.

We can avail ourselves of the joy and peace that come from God when we avoid sin and seek God. God is just and worthy of praise. God judges those who do evil and blesses those who are righteous.

• When have you been distressed, as David was, asking questions of God?

• How do you see these psalms being relevant to your life today?

Road Signs

• **Selah:** This word occurs many times throughout the Book of Psalms. The exact meaning of the word is unknown, but it is believed to be a musical term.
• **Psalter:** This alternative name for the Book of Psalms could also be used for a collection of psalms for worship or devotional use.

Prayer

Thank you, God, for these psalms. Inspire me to be mindful of the many ways in which you uphold me and care for me. Amen.

The Earliest Blog
Psalms 11–21

 Scouting the Terrain

Seventy-three of the psalms have David's name attached to them. We know that David was a skilled musician, as he was commissioned, while still a young boy, to play his harp for King Saul. We know that he danced in the streets, much to the chagrin of his wife Michal, and sang praises to God when the ark was brought to Jerusalem. One needs only look at the comprehensive list of Temple musicians in 1 Chronicles 25 to see the importance David gave to music in worship.

Trailblazer
• David

Fourteen of David's psalms relate directly to events in his life. Psalm 18, for instance, talks about God delivering him from the hands of Saul and his other enemies. Many of the other psalms reflect David's admiration for and trust in God as his Sustainer, Protector, and Deliverer.

• What have you learned about David as you read more of his heart poured out in these psalms?

• In what ways do you praise God? cry out to God?

2. **NOW READ PSALMS 11–21.**

3 Switchback

Those who truly trust in God have no reason for panic, no matter what the circumstances. Even when it seems that evil is all around us and may even be defeating us, we know that God is in control and will bring justice to the righteous. Occasionally, bad things happen or we have to endure some tough circumstances. Sometimes it can seem as though even God has abandoned us. That, of course, is not the case, and we can become close to God again through prayer. The person who trusts God possesses deep abiding joy, strength, and security, which comfort immediately and for eternity.

Psalm 15 focuses on the requirements for those who will enter God's holy presence at the sanctuary. Notice the emphasis on personal holiness and moral uprightness. This requirement has not changed for 21st century believers; however, we have an intercessor who is perfectly holy and perfectly righteous to enter God's presence on our behalf. Those who put their faith in Christ Jesus as Lord and Savior have fulfilled these requirements and can enjoy God's presence now and for eternity.

• With which verses from today's reading can you most identify? How do they apply to you?

• How does Psalm 15 affect the way you approach the worship of God?

4 Prayer

God, my deliverer, thank you for upholding me in times of trouble. Help me more fully rely on you. Amen.

Who God Is
Psalms 22–31

① Scouting the Terrain

Trailblazer
• David

Psalm 22 is recognized as a Messianic prophecy. David is being attacked by his enemies and cries out to God, feeling abandoned ("My God, my God, why have you forsaken me?"). In the New Testament, we read the same cry from Jesus. David's experience was a shadow of Christ's experience of total abandonment to come. The psalm prophesies the things that Jesus will endure: "All who see me mock at me"; "all my bones are out of joint"; "for my clothing they cast lots." As the psalm concludes, though, it's apparent that this is not the end but the beginning; because "future generations will be told about the Lord, and proclaim his deliverance to a people yet unborn, saying that he has done it." In his dying moments, Jesus offered us hope by referring to this psalm.

• What gives you hope to make it through tough times?

• Why is possessing hope important?

• Do you know someone who seems to feel hopeless? Describe that person's outlook on God and life. What message of hope can you give that person?

② NOW READ PSALMS 22–31.

3 Switchback

Taken together, Psalms 22, 23, and 24 outline all that Jesus is. First, he is our Savior, the once-and-for-all sacrifice for our sins. Second, he is the Good Shepherd, who leads us on the pathway of righteousness and protects us from evil. Third, he is the Almighty King, worthy of our adoration and praise.

When we recall the stories of David, we remember that he was often in mortal danger. Even as a small boy, he was fighting off lions and bears that would attack his sheep. As he ran from Saul and from Absalom, his life was often at stake. In his distress, David turned to God, with the confidence that God was listening to him, was looking after him, and would deliver him. David turned to God, where he found love, forgiveness, and guidance. David always concluded his prayers of distress with praises for God. When our lives are beginning to unravel, we, too, can be confident that our God hears us and will protect us.

• When you praise God, what happens to your fear, doubt, and distress?

• How can you become more confident of God's protecting love in your life?

4 Prayer

Protector God, be near me. Help me feel your hand upholding me when life presents its challenges. Amen.

Psalms 22 and 41 contain prophecies about Jesus' crucifixion. Read through this week's assigned psalms, identifying other Messianic prophecies. Take a quiz at *amazingbiblerace.com* to see how much you've learned.

The Weight of Sin
Psalms 32–36

1 Scouting the Terrain

Sin brings with it some emotional burdens, such as guilt and grief. The longer we carry around our sin, the heavier we are burdened.

Trailblazer
• David

Imagine carrying around a heavy rock all day, having to bear its weight without rest. How good will it feel when you are able to put it down? David speaks about how confession gives this same kind of relief from the burden of sin. When we confess our sins, express remorse for them, and make changes to avoid repeating them, God willingly and freely gives us forgiveness.

God's righteousness, justice, and unfailing love are lifted up in today's psalms. God's Word is forever true, and God's works are wonderful. God watches over us and guides us. God is truly worthy of our praise.

• When have you identified and confessed a habitual sin? How did it feel to be free of the burden of that sin?

• In Psalm 32, how does David describe the benefit(s) of confession and repentance?

2 NOW READ PSALMS 32–36.

3 Switchback

Having a good relationship with God is not the same thing as having a "get out of jail free card" when it comes to times of trouble and grief. But those who walk with God do not walk alone through these trying times. As David writes, "Many are the afflictions of the righteous, but the LORD rescues them from them all" (Psalm 34:19).

Those who seek God "feast abundantly" or "lack no good thing" (34:10). They are richly blessed. Meanwhile, the evildoers are "thrust down, unable to rise."

• When things are going wrong, what are some things that you do to feel closer to God?

• When you consider David's experiences (struggles, fear, sins) and the way he lived his life, how do you view his writing? Is he a credible writer about God? Why, or why not?

4 Prayer

Merciful God, I confess much sin to you. Forgive me and enable me to walk in your ways. Amen.

Joy Deep Down in My Heart
Psalms 37–41

1 Scouting the Terrain

David says, in Psalm 39, that a lifetime spent gathering up wealth is meaningless, because you can't take it with you and you have no control over who gets it when you're gone. (This sentiment is echoed in the Book of Ecclesiastes, which some say was written by David's son, Solomon.) David emphasizes the brevity of life in this psalm. David's painful struggle is evident, but his reliance on the Lord for hope and salvation is also prominent.

Trailblazer
• David

Those aspects of life on Earth, which seem so important (wealth, material possessions, and social status), are inconsequential when viewed from God's perspective. Our working to acquire earthly possessions is a vain exercise. David's prayer is to have his hope in God renewed. He prays to God for reason to rejoice again.

• When have your material possessions failed to give you reason to rejoice?

• Does considering the briefness of your life draw you closer to God? Why, or why not?

2 NOW READ PSALMS 37–41.

③ Switchback

An old saying goes, "Money can't buy happiness." The saying is wrong. Money can, in fact, buy you a lot of things that will make you happy: a new video game, new shoes, or dinner and a movie. Happiness is only temporary, though. Sooner or later, you'll grow bored with the video game, the shoes will wear out, and you'll forget about the movie. Perhaps the saying should be, "Money can't buy joy." Joy, unlike happiness, endures. It's an abiding emotion that comes from knowing that God secures your future. Joy comes from knowing that this Earth is a temporary stop on to your ultimate destination: eternity with the Lord. When Jesus reminds us to store up for ourselves treasures in Heaven, he knows that the pleasures of this life are only temporary.

• Can you think of something that, at first, made you really happy, but now seems like no big deal?

• In what ways has God given you joy?

Water Break

It's time for another break. Catch your breath and rest your legs. You've made a great start in the Psalms. It may not be quite like running with your MP3 player, but you're singing the songs of the Bible. Keep going!

Road Signs

• **Handbreadth:** This is one of the smallest measures in the Hebrew system, probably the width of four fingers at their base.

④ Prayer

God of abiding joy, Help me find lasting joy in heavenly treasures. Amen.

Filled and Led
Psalms 42–48

Scouting the Terrain

The second book of the Psalter (Psalms 42–72) opens with nine psalms that are credited to the "Sons of Korah," who were the Temple singers. It's obvious in a few of these verses that the writer no longer has access to the Temple. He lived in the north and was cut off when Israel split after Solomon's death. It is not unusual for Hebrew scripture to be written to preserve or remember what had been. There was a time when God was present with Israel in the corporate sense. Not only is it possible that the psalmist is longing for God in his own heart but is also longing for the very presence of God in the communal sense.

Trailblazers

• **Sons of Korah**

While the psalms in the first book were more personal in nature, those in the second and third books take on a more national theme. Psalm 44 is written in response to a stunning military defeat. The psalmist recalls how God had led their ancestors to victory after victory, but now they have been defeated by their enemy. The psalm highlights that one should not trust in his or her weapons or strength. Victory comes from God alone.

• Can you think of a song that has captured the feelings of the entire country, if not at least a large group of your friends? If so, what is it?

• How does God equip you to "battle" victoriously?

2. NOW READ PSALMS 42–48.

Switchback

Psalm 46 affirms the benefit of trusting in the Lord in the middle of extreme adversity. The psalmist speaks with confidence because he knows that God is with him. The words of Psalm 46:10, " 'Be still, and know that I am God!' " remind us that the proper response to a great, powerful, holy God is submissive respect and silence. Contrast verse 10 with verse 6. The nations who roared just a few verses earlier are still and quiet now in the presence of God.

• Do you have a time each day when you are "still" before God? What does this look like?

• Describe how you think your nation appears to God (in uproar or being still). What would happen if the nation was more often still before God?

• When you face struggles, are you confident that God will hear your prayers and help you? Why, or why not? What do you need to help you live more confidently in God?

Prayer

Dear God, please make me confident that you are with me. Help me be still and feel your presence. Amen.

Pace Pusher

Martin Luther was inspired by Psalm 46 to write his famous hymn "A Mighty Fortress Is Our God." Compare the psalm with the hymn. Blog about your observations.

Rich and Perfect
Psalms 49–55

1 Scouting the Terrain

"Are you living for God or for gold?" is the question posed in Psalm 49. Echoing the wisdom contained in previous psalms, the message here is that life does not last forever and no amount of riches can buy an extension. Those who trust in themselves and rely on their riches will perish, but those who trust in God have more to look forward to: "God will ransom my soul . . . for he will receive me." God has ransomed our souls, with the sacrifice of Jesus. So the question becomes, "Are you living for today or for tomorrow?" The wealth, power, and prestige we work for today cannot buy us everlasting life tomorrow. Only a new life in Christ offers everlasting life for countless tomorrows.

Trailblazers

- **David**
- **Sons of Korah**

• Why is the promise of everlasting life important as you live this life?

• The psalmist writes of the prosperity of the rich and the reality of death. How do you see these themes relevant to your life today?

2 NOW READ PSALMS 49–55.

3 Switchback

We see right into David's heart as we read Psalm 51, which he wrote after Nathan confronted him about the situation with Bathsheba (2 Samuel 11–12). David confesses his sin and asks to be cleansed. He asks God to change his heart so that he will stay pure. Then he says that he will tell others of God's grace and mercy.

David was not perfect, but he sought God fervently—even more so when he was in the shadow of sin. He trusted God many times when things were bad. It sure would have been easy to lose faith when Ahithophel, his friend and his most trusted advisor, betrayed him (Psalm 55). David and his friend had worshiped together. David feels the pain of a broken relationship. David remains strong, though, writing, "Cast your burden on the Lord, and he will sustain you" (verse 22).

• How does it feel to confess your sin to God?

• When have you been betrayed by a close friend? How does David's hope in the Lord (verses 22-23) encourage you during difficult times in your relationships?

4 Prayer

Dear God, thank you for forgiving my sins. Create in me a clean heart. Amen.

Compare and contrast David's suffering in Psalm 55 with the suffering of another New Testament man (read Matthew 26:47-56). Go to *amazingbiblerace.com* and take a quiz about the two passages.

Road Signs

• **Sheol:** This Hebrew word means "abode of the dead." It was thought to be a dark, gloomy, and dusty place deep within the earth. When you see the word *Sheol* in the Scripture, like in Psalm 49, it might be helpful to substitute the words "dead" or "death" as you read.

Fear Itself
Psalms 56–61

1 Scouting the Terrain

Trailblazer
• David

What are you afraid of? Many people are afraid of spiders and snakes. Some are afraid of heights or flying or dogs. Comedian Jerry Seinfeld once said that the number one thing people were afraid of was public speaking. Many people are more afraid to talk in front of a crowd than they are of death. According to Seinfeld, that means that at a funeral, people would rather be the corpse than the eulogist.

Today's readings are about fear—specifically, David's fear. David had plenty to be afraid of. There was the time he fought Goliath, the time he was running from Saul, and the time it looked like he was going to lose the whole kingdom to Absalom. Again, his incredible faith shines through. David's confidence that the Lord will save him echoes throughout the Psalms. David has God on his side. What can mere mortals do to him? Even if he loses everything he has, he still has God, in whom he can take refuge.

• What makes you afraid?

• When have you had to face one of your fears? How did you do it?

• How can our faith in God help us face our fears?

2 NOW READ PSALMS 56–61.

3 Switchback

Psalm 59 has an interesting back story. To get the complete picture, reread 1 Samuel 19:11-17. (You read it in Leg 2.) It's before David assumes the throne. David is married to Michal, who is Saul's daughter. Saul (David's father-in-law) sends men to David's house to kill him. But Michal helps her husband escape by lowering him down from a window.

Despite his fear, David prays to God for deliverance and protection. He keeps his focus on God, not on his enemy. In verse 9, David's confidence is evident as he prays expectantly. He believes that God will act on his behalf.

• When you are afraid or worried, where is your focus—on God or on your enemy?

• How would you rate your confidence level that God will protect you in times of fear (1 = not confident at all, 5 = somewhat confident, 10 = extremely confident)?

• Think of a fearful or difficult situation you are facing. Now, read Psalm 56, substituting your situation throughout the psalm. Pray Psalm 56 in this manner whenever you feel anxious or afraid.

fast forward

Many of the psalms are songs of praise or songs of lament. With your team, choose a universal concern to teens. Just as David did, your team will compose and perform a psalm (song) so that others can identify with you, while you point others to God's goodness. Post a video of your team performing your song, a music video of your song, or a podcast featuring the song and interviews about the song's creation on *amazingbiblerace.com* for points.

4 Prayer

God, please help me not be afraid. Convince me of your protective and abiding love. Amen.

Hungry? Thirsty?
Psalms 62–67

WEEK
5
◇
DAY
4

1 Scouting the Terrain

Throughout his psalms, David expresses a confidence that God loves and protects him. Note how David describes his love for the Lord in Psalm 63. He says he seeks God, he thirsts for God. He describes God's love as better than life and he's satisfied as with a rich feast.

Trailblazer

• **David**

• Think of your favorite meal. Would you describe your relationship with God as being as satisfying to your soul as a cheeseburger (or whatever your favorite food is) quiets your growling tummy?

• How would you answer the question, "What's life to you?"

• What really satisfies you?

• How can you pray for a heart for God that mirrors David's heart in Psalm 63?

2 NOW READ PSALMS 62–67.

54

3 Switchback

Psalms 65, 66, and 67 have similar themes. They offer thanksgiving and adoration. They ask for blessing, and they praise God for provision:

- Praise God who creates nature, nurtures it, and uses it to sustain us.
- Praise God who leads us through times of trial and delivers us into times of peace.
- Praise God for hearing our prayers and loving us unconditionally.
- Praise God for the many blessings in our lives.
- Praise God just because God is worthy of praise.

Most of the time we are too self-consumed to thank God for all of the good gifts in our lives. We see all the wonderful things around us, but rarely stop to admire their Creator. We experience all the good things happening to us, but often just consider ourselves to be lucky. God commands our praise and is worthy of our praise—for the beautiful sunset, or the wonderful friends in our lives, or the promise of salvation. We were made for worship.

- What can you praise God for?

- Why is it good that we praise God?

4 Prayer

Creator God, please give me an attitude of gratitude so that I may praise you for your wonderful gifts. Amen.

Consistency
Psalms 68–72

① Scouting the Terrain

How do you know that the sun will come up tomorrow morning? Is it because it came up today and yesterday? The sun has a pretty decent track record. So when morning arrives tomorrow, we can certainly assume that the sun will be there. God has a spotless track record, too. God promised to deliver Noah through the storm. God promised Abraham that his descendants would outnumber the stars in the sky. God promised the Israelites deliverance from slavery into the Promised Land. God promised David an everlasting kingdom, which was the coming of the Messiah. God has never left a promise unfulfilled. So we can believe in God. When God promises never to abandon us, we can believe it. When God promises us eternal life in heaven, we can count on it. God is forever faithful, which allows us to have full faith in God. This is the faith that the psalmists are singing about, that no matter how bad things seem, God is our rock, our anchor, our foothold, and our deliverer.

Trailblazers
- **David**
- **Solomon**

• What does God's being a promise keeper mean for our faith?

• How do you understand God's faithfulness in your life?

• What does it mean for you when you don't recognize or "feel" God's faithfulness?

WEEK
5
◆
DAY
5

② NOW READ PSALMS 68–72.

③ Switchback

The final psalm in the second book of the Psalter is credited to Solomon. This psalm was probably used to celebrate his coronation or its anniversary. Psalm 72 petitions God to bless the just king with prosperity. Solomon ruled Israel during its peak. The nation was at peace, secure against its enemies. Solomon had wisdom beyond compare and rulers of other nations sought audience with him. Neither before, nor after, did the nation prosper so. Reread Psalm 72, looking for words that anticipate the coming of another King.

• In what ways might Psalm 72 be talking about the coming of the Messiah?

• Which verses from today's reading can you most identify with? How do they apply to you?

Water Break

You're finished with Book II of the Psalms. Good job! What is God teaching you as you run this race? Are you excited to learn even more?

Keep going. There are more psalms ahead.

④ Prayer

Dear God, thank you for the opportunity to study these psalms. Inspire me by the faith of the psalm writers. Help me continue to reflect upon these readings so that I might grow closer to you. Amen.

Prayer in a Minor Key
Psalms 73–77

 Scouting the Terrain

Book III of the psalter (Psalms 73–89) begins in a minor key. All too often the wicked prosper—so much so that the upright sometimes wonder why they bother to lead pure lives (73:13-14).

Trailblazer

• Asaph

Arrogance, brutality, and blasphemy go unpunished; and nowhere do the psalm singers see this state of affairs more clearly than in the Babylonians' destruction of the Temple in 587 B.C. (74:1-11). Those who trust God can feel abandoned in the darkest of times; the very thought of God can provoke "groans" (77:3).

How should God's people handle tough times? First, they should follow the psalm singers' example and tell God exactly how they feel. These psalms ultimately find hope for the future because they remember what God has done in the past. Psalm 74 recalls the great, cosmic battle God waged in the beginning of time against the forces of chaos. God won that conflict. So how much more will God defeat mere mortal foes (74:12-23)?

Sixteenth-century Protestant reformer John Calvin believed that the psalter's greatest lesson for us was how to bear adversity in godly ways. These psalms show practical strategies used by saints before us to move from the minor key to the major—from sorrow about life's pain to celebration about God's promises.

• How do you remain committed to leading a godly life when godlessness seems to go unpunished?

• To what acts of God in the past do you look in order to find hope and strength for facing the present and the future?

2 **NOW READ PSALMS 73–77.**

3 Switchback

You've seen in today's psalms that a strong memory of what God has done for God's people in the past can lead them to trust that God will act on their behalf in the future. God chooses "the set time that I appoint" (75:2a); our task is to wait with faith and courage.

Waiting, however, doesn't necessarily mean doing nothing. Critics of Christianity sometimes claim that faith encourages passivity in the face of injustice and evil. They assume a sort of shoulder-shrugging, "What can I do? God will take care of it someday" attitude that relieves people of taking any responsibility for making the world a better place.

The individuals who first sang these psalms may not, in fact, have been in any position to work for change, particularly after Babylon conquered Judah. But they did what they could: They prayed. Sometimes, we say "All we can do is pray" as a way of resigning ourselves to what seems inevitable. We too often forget that prayer, at its best, *is* "doing something." As the apostle James writes, "The prayer of the righteous is powerful and effective" (James 5:16b).

- When have you said or been tempted to say, "All we can do is pray"?

Road Signs

- **Salem** (76:2): This is another form of the word *Jerusalem,* which means "peace," as you can hear in the ancient and modern Hebrew word *shalom.*

- How can you *pray to* God and *act for* God in a difficult situation that you or someone else is facing?

4 Prayer

God, move me from sorrow about life's pain to celebration about your promises. Amen.

History Repeats?
Psalms 78–83

1 Scouting the Terrain

Do you watch the news or read the news in a newspaper or on the Internet? Most American youth don't. But as you know, your generation does care about current events and significant issues.

The psalms you read today demonstrate the importance of knowing about the world at large. Repeatedly, the psalm singers cry out to God because of "the nations." The nations have attacked and defeated Israel (79:6-7). The nations plot against God (83:5-8) and, in fact, declare divine status for themselves. The nations act in pride and arrogance, trampling society's most vulnerable members (82:1-5). Yes, the psalm singers are paying attention to the world—and they don't like what they see.

Trailblazer

• **Asaph**

Swiss pastor and theologian Karl Barth said Christians should live with the newspaper in one hand and the Bible in the other. Faith reminds us that the same nations who are causing so much pain and distress will ultimately be accountable to God, to whom all nations belong (82:8; 83:18). The God who "drove out the nations" before Israel in the past (80:8) will again exercise divine authority and will turn all bad news into good.

• How much attention to do you pay to world news? Why?

• What distresses you about the behavior of "the nations" today?

• How do you pray for other nations of the world? for our own?

2 NOW READ PSALMS 78–83.

③ Switchback

The psalm singers also drew negative lessons from the past, as we discover today in Psalm 78. Although the psalm recounts Israelite triumphs, it also highlights how Israel's ancestors proved themselves to be "a stubborn and rebellious generation ... whose spirit was not faithful to God" (78:8). The past demands interpretation. Sometimes, those interpretations inspire and reassure; at others, they challenge and motivate us to do better. (Contrast also psalms 15 and 106.) We need to view the past from both perspectives in order to live the present as the people God calls us to be.

• When you think back over your relationship with God, do you find that story primarily comforting or primarily challenging? What about the stories of your family and your congregation's past?

• How would looking at these stories in another way affect your present and future relationship with God today?

Psalms

Road Signs

• **Zoan** (ZOH-an): The Pharaohs of Egypt lived in Zoan from the eleventh to eighth centuries B.C.
• **Shiloh:** When the Israelites first entered the Promised Land, Shiloh (pronounced SHY-low) was the central place of worship until the Philistines captured the Ark of the Covenant, which never returned to that place (1 Samuel 4)—an event this psalm attributes to God's own doing, as an expression of divine displeasure.
• **"The one whom you made strong for yourself"**: The psalm singer apparently means the king of Israel. A more literal translation, however, reads, "The son of man whom..." (NIV). Remembering that Jesus called himself the Son of Man, then, Christians have sometimes taken this verse as a messianic prophecy.

④ Prayer

God, give me wise eyes to interpret my past and anticipate the future. Amen.

Tell Me How You Really Feel
Psalms 84–89

Scouting the Terrain

On Day 1 of this week, the psalms showed how expressing our true feelings to God, even such emotions as fear and anger, can lead to personal renewal and hope. One of today's readings, however, teaches that strengthened faith and confidence for the future do not always come right away. Psalm 88 is the only psalm of lament that does not end with a note of praise or a promise of brighter days to come. It's the exception, not the rule—but it's an important exception.

Many expressions of Christianity in modern America emphasize the positive benefits of a relationship with God. Yes, those benefits are many. But when we describe our faith only as "joyful," "peaceful," or "fulfilling," we risk reducing the gospel to "warm and fuzzy" optimism; and we misrepresent God as hearing only the prayers of the happy and contented.

God hears us even when we are hurt, angry, and scared; and God values our prayers during hard times as much as when we pray to praise or thank God.

Trailblazers

• **David**
• **Sons of Korah**

• How deeply can you relate to the singer of Psalm 88?

• Do you ever "self-censor" your prayers? Why, or why not?

• How will Psalm 88 affect your personal prayer life?

2. NOW READ PSALMS 84–89.

3 Switchback

Images of the monarchy are prominent in the first and last psalms for today's reading. Psalm 84 includes a plea for God to strengthen the king, who is God's "anointed" (verse 9). Psalm 89 talks about the king more extensively; specifically, King David.

God wants us to pray for leaders and governmental authorities (see 1 Timothy 2:3). Whether we live in a "blue state" or a "red state," whether we agree with our elected officials' policies or not, we, as Christians, have the responsibility to pray for them, to pray that God will bless them with wisdom to know what is right and the courage to do it. We Americans don't live under a monarchy; but our prayers, like those of the psalm singers, should include intercessions (prayers or requests to God on behalf of others) for those to whom we have entrusted the authority to govern.

• How will you pray for your local, state, and national elected officials today?

Road Signs

• **The Valley of Baca** (BAY-cuh): Although scholars have not yet pinpointed Baca on a map, they do know that the Hebrew word comes from the verb meaning "to drip." Logically then the valley of Baca, wherever it was, would have been an appropriate place for falling tears.

• **"He's Got the Whole World . . ."** (Psalm 87): In verse 4, these nations ("Egypt and Babylon, also Philistia, even Tyre, along with Cush [Ethiopia]") are not generally seen in a favorable light in Scripture. Here, however, they are said to be nations that acknowledge God and that will eventually claim Mount Zion itself as their birthplace. This is a profound statement that God rules—and loves—all peoples and nations.

4 Prayer

Lord God, please help me pray faithfully for my leaders. Protect those in charge and give them wisdom to lead. Amen.

Under the Care of God's Hands
Psalms 90–100

1 Scouting the Terrain

Today's psalms have a way of really putting us in our place. The psalter is in some ways among the most human-centered portions of Scripture. Each of these poems features the voices of human beings speaking about their experience in emotional terms. The psalms are human speech to God. At the same time, the psalms, by the Spirit, become God's speech to humans.

Trailblazers

• **Various psalmists**

In these passages we read constant reminders of God's greatness, majesty, and immortality, which highlight our vulnerability and frailty when compared to the God who is sovereign over all.

The supreme ruler celebrated in these songs, the divine executor of justice, the creator of the cosmos and all that is in them—this God and no other, the one true God is pledged to us now and eternally (see Psalm 91:14-16). This God teaches us how to live and promises never to reject us (see Psalm 94:14). This God cares for us as a shepherd cares for the flock (see Psalms 95:6-7 and 100:3). Saturating our hearts and minds in the language of the psalms better equips us to express gratitude and praise for such unfathomable love.

• What images of God or language about God from today's reading especially grab your attention? Why?

2 NOW READ PSALMS 90–100.

3 Switchback

Psalm 90 ends with a plea for God to "prosper for us the work of our hands" (90:17). Before we can ask God to bless our handiwork, however, we must seriously consider what our handiwork is. How do we use our hands? To hurt or to help? To wound or to heal? To tear down or to build up? The psalm singers' words are not a kind of "blanket blessing," asking God to smile upon whatever we choose to do; rather, we need to commit to using our hands as instruments of grace—as were the outstretched, nail-scarred hands of Jesus Christ.

• Spend some time looking at your hands. How are you using them to do God's work today?

As you read from Psalm 73 through Psalm 106, look for references to the topics below. When you've studied the passages, take a quiz online at *amazingbiblerace.com* to match the topics with their references.

• foolish ideas about God
• the Temple in Jerusalem
• a plea for God to act with justice
• psalms of lamentation to God
• psalms about Israel's history with God
• God and "the nations"
• sea monsters that symbolize chaos
• human mortality
• celebrations of God's sovereignty

4 Prayer

God, I commit my hands to you as instruments of grace. Prosper the work of my hands. Amen.

Creation: Can't Live Without It
Psalms 101–106

Scouting the Terrain

We humans have a tough time forgiving. We often think that forgiveness means pretending that nothing ever happened, saying that our feelings weren't actually hurt, allowing people to continue to use and abuse us. God says, though, that forgiveness means none of these things. But it does mean, at some level, letting go. To forgive is to make a radical choice: to refuse to let the wrongs inflicted upon us define who we are.

Trailblazers

- David
- An afflicted man

As atrocious as some of the things we human beings do to one another are, none of them can, in the end, compare to the wrongs we have done God by turning our back on our gracious creator and savior (see Psalm 106, for example). But does God allow those wrongs to "set the terms" of our relationship? No! Psalm 103 contains one of the grandest proclamations of grace in Scripture (verse 12). God forgives and forgets.

- Whom do you find it hard, if not impossible, to forgive?

- How can reflecting on God's forgiveness of you in Jesus Christ affect your decision to forgive that person?

Road Signs

- **Leviathan** (luh-VIGH-uh-thun): This creature, mentioned in Psalm 104:26 and in Job 41:1, may be what we would call a whale. However, scholars of ancient literature point out that Leviathan occurs in eastern mythology as a powerful sea dragon, the embodiment of chaos. The fact that, according to this psalm, God has reduced Leviathan to a playful ocean animal speaks volumes about the power of God over creation and serves as a symbol of God's creative ability.

Switchback

Psalm 104 celebrates God's good gift of the creation. The psalm singer pays loving attention to mountains and valleys, birds and beasts, day and night—the world whirls around us as we read this song, and all we can do is say, "Amen!" to the central declaration, "O LORD, how manifold are your works! In wisdom you have made them all; the earth is full of your creatures" (104:24).

God has given us a wonderful world indeed, and it is our responsibility as people of faith to ensure we preserve it for generations to come.

• What practical steps do you take or can you take to help preserve the manifold, wonderful works of the Lord in creation?

NOW READ PSALMS 101–106.

 This week's psalms singer attempts to interpret events of the past by shaping events, people, and places into a "plot" that proclaims God's purposes.

With your team, compile a scrapbook or "family album" that interprets what God has done in your past. How has God dealt with you, your family, your youth ministry, or your congregation in the past? And what do you learn about the past for the future?

Upload digital files of your scrapbook to *amazingbiblerace.com* to receive points.

 Prayer

God, forgive me as I forgive those who have sinned against me. Amen.

Water Break

It's not every racer who gets to sing while she or he runs. But in this leg of the Amazing Bible Race, you've been doing just that: joining your voice with the chorus of the faithful from the past. So keep running and keep singing, learning the language of faith on which you can rely as you race with God, following Jesus, through all your days!

The Soundtrack of Your Life
Psalms 107–118

 ## Scouting the Terrain

Psalms 113–118, from today's reading, have been treated for centuries in Judaism as a "soundtrack" for God's people. These psalms are the *Hallel,* or "praise." Observant Jews recite, often from memory, these seven psalms during many festivals, including Passover. Scholars don't know how long this practice has gone on or whether these psalms have always been kept together. But it's possible that even in Jesus' day, these psalms were a traditional part of celebrating Passover.

Trailblazers

- David
- Various psalmists

What's certain is that these psalms helped Jesus' disciples understand and express their master's mission. In Psalm 118, for instance, we hear about a stone rejected by mortals but exalted by God—a symbol used in the New Testament for Jesus (Acts 4:11; 1 Peter 2:7), including by Jesus himself (Matthew 21:42).

As you read Book V of the psalter (Psalms 107-150), make them, like the rest, part of your "playlist," your "soundtrack." Live your life to the accompaniment of God's music, and discover—as did Jesus' first followers—who you are in God's sight and who God calls you to be.

- What are your favorite songs? Why?

- What's the "genre" of your personal spiritual soundtrack: hip-hop? the blues? country songs? Broadway show tunes? hard rock? folk songs? Explain.

2. NOW READ PSALMS 107–118.

Switchback

Psalm 107 takes us on a whirlwind tour of sandy deserts, gloomy prisons, and stormy oceans. People in these circumstances might make any number of choices—but the people of whom the psalm sings all make the same choice, the only right choice: "Then they cried to the LORD...."

When we face "adventures" we'd rather not experience, when we have tough times, we could choose to panic, show fear, or just give up. But those choices all lead to a bad end. The only good choice is to "cry to the LORD." God might not instantly give us a happy ending; but God will hear our cry. God promises to guide us through all the choices that still lie before us.

• What difficult choice(s) are you facing today?

• How will you "cry to the LORD" about your decision?

Prayer

God, I want to praise you. I want to discover your call for my life. Amen.

A Legal Alphabet
Psalm 119

Scouting the Terrain

You've probably heard about wacky laws that are reportedly still on the books—like the Tennessee law that forbids using a lasso to catch fish, or the Massachusetts law against having a gorilla in the back seat of any car. And believe it or not, it's allegedly illegal in Quitman, Georgia, for a chicken to cross the road (Is it illegal to tell jokes in Quitman?); however, in Arcadia, California, peacocks have the right of way to cross any street.

These laws do, however, emphasize our view of law as something that limits instead of liberates, something that restricts instead of refreshes. That's why Psalm 119 may surprise us: It is a love song—to the Law.

Trailblazer

• An unknown psalmist

The psalm singer knows that true freedom is found by living within God's Law. The Law was and is God's gift to Israel, to all humanity; it's an outline of the boundaries inside of which real, abundant life can be realized.

And so we, like the psalm singer, should strive to obey—not to make God love us, but because God already loves us! "The earth, O LORD, is full of your steadfast love; teach me your statutes" (verse 64).

• Have you ever broken a law or a major rule? What happened? How would things have turned out differently had you obeyed?

• Have you ever had to "lay down the law" to a child or someone else in need of guidance? If so, how was the experience similar to God's gift of the Law?

• How grateful are you for God's Law? Why are you, or why are you not?

NOW READ PSALM 119.

③ Switchback

Our first response is to bristle at any law. After all, we cherish our freedom and independence. But the psalm singer tells a different story. The psalm singer writes of suffering at the hands of enemies; God's Law is all that is keeping her or him from giving up completely: "This is my comfort in my distress, that your promise gives me life" (verse 50). And he or she does not really claim to obey God perfectly; near the beginning, the psalm singer prays, "O that my ways may be steadfast" (verse 5), suggesting that they are not always so. This psalm singer is trying to live up to God's ideals but is aware that "all have sinned" (see Romans 3:23), so the writer relies on God. Psalm 119 is meant to inspire us to ask God to help us be more faithful in the future.

• When have you viewed God's laws as oppressive?

• When have you viewed God's laws as comforting and life-giving?

Psalm 119 was written in the form of an acrostic poem, a poem in which each section or verse begins with a different letter of the alphabet. Sometimes the letters spell a word. In this case, the poem has 22 sections, one for each letter of the Hebrew alphabet. Formal prayers such as Psalm 119 serve to give us words with which to pray when we find it hard to think of our own. Forms such as Psalm 119's acrostic sometimes make us think before we voice our words to God.

Work as a team to write an acrostic prayer, using every letter of our alphabet. Have all of your team members participate in reading it for a video. Upload your video to *amazingbiblerace.com* to earn points.

④ Prayer

Lord, help me see that your Law is a gift. Give me love for your Law. Amen.

Psalms

Changes of Perspective
Psalms 120–130

1 Scouting the Terrain

Psalms 120–134 are identified as "songs of ascents." Scholars don't agree on exactly what that identification means; but some theorize that pilgrims sang these songs on their way to the Temple in Jerusalem, that place above all places where ancient Israelites expected to encounter God. In fact, some early rabbis pointed out that, just as the Temple had fifteen steps, this mini-psalter includes fifteen psalms. Notice how these songs present people approaching God in a wide range of moods, from despondent to joyful.

Worship is not about how we feel or what we can "get out of it." We worship God because God is worthy to be praised. No matter how we happen to be feeling, and no matter what circumstances we find ourselves in, we can—in the traditional communion prayer's language—"lift up our hearts" and "ascend" to God. Feelings and circumstances change; but through all those changes, God keeps us close. God travels with us and will "keep [our] going out and [our] coming in from this time on and forevermore" (Psalm 121:8).

WEEK
7
◆
DAY
3

Trailblazers
- David
- Solomon
- An unknown psalmist

• What music do you choose to listen to or sing when you travel? Why?

• When has the image of life as a pilgrimage or journey felt most real to you?

• How can you increase your awareness of God as a traveling companion?

2 NOW READ PSALMS 120–130.

3 Switchback

One reason many interpreters think that the "songs of ascents" were pilgrimage music is that so many of them make references to "going up," as travelers would go up from the Judean countryside to Jerusalem. For example, Psalm 121 sounds as though it could have been sung by people who see the holy city (their destination) atop a mountain while they are at a lower elevation.

Psalm 130, however, makes a clearly metaphorical reference to depths and heights; but it is not "just" symbolic language. The words express a powerful emotional reality: the psalm singer is in "the depths"—he or she is drowning in chaos and darkness, including the darkness of his or her own sin. But the psalm singer maintains faith in the God who proved, long ago at Creation, to be the One who can control the depths, who can bring order out of disorder, who can command light to shine in the darkness (see Genesis 1).

• How have you experienced "the depths" in your life?

• How has God lifted you out of the depths? Or are you still waiting to ascend?

4 Prayer

Lord God, I praise you for bringing me from the depths and allowing me to ascend to new life in Christ. Amen.

You Praise God With That Mouth?
Psalms 131–139

1 Scouting the Terrain

Through the prophet Jeremiah, God asks, "The heart is devious above all else....Who can understand it?" (Jeremiah 17:9). Good question! We sinful and broken human beings can't understand it on our own, as today's psalms illustrate. The psalm singer feels very near to God—as close as a baby to its mother (Psalm 131); surrounded by God "behind and before" (Psalm 139:5)—but it is just then when bitterness and hatred show themselves. The psalm singer declares, "My heart is not lifted up" (131:1) but later states, "I hate [God's enemies] with perfect hatred" (139:22). Aren't those proud, haughty words? Well, maybe.

Sure, the psalm singers may not always be as pure of heart as they seem to think they are or as we think they should have been—but, of course, we know that we're not, either. Instead of criticizing the psalm singers, we would do better to follow their example and leave the job of judging our heart to God, the only One who can do it properly (Psalm 139:23-24)! We can be encouraged, too, to see God's mercy in the middle of their sin, knowing that God will deal graciously with us.

- How true is it that the times we feel closest to God can also be the times when we are most tempted to sin?

- How have you struggled with feelings of self-righteousness in your relationships with God and other people?

- When you see sin in someone else's life, what is your reaction?

Trailblazers

- David
- An unknown psalmist

WEEK
7
◆
DAY
4

2 NOW READ PSALMS 131–139.

74

3 Switchback

Another antiphonal psalm (remember, for example, Psalm 80), Psalm 136 is sometimes, in Judaism, called the "Great Hallel"—the great praise! From before creation, through the Exodus, to present providence, the psalm traces God's many expressions of mercy to the chosen people. Each episode proves God's love.

The psalm anticipates a later Jewish prayer, the *Dayenu*. Sung at Passover, the Dayenu recites God's gifts to Israel—deliverance from Egypt, the parting of the Sea, the giving of the Law, and more—stating after each gift, "It would have been enough." Had God done only this for us, it would have been enough… but God also did this!

God's grace toward us bears repeating—again and again! How many times do God's people need to tell the world? There is no limit!

• How has God repeatedly shown to you that God's "steadfast love endures forever"?

Road Signs

• **Ephrathah** (EF-ruh-thuh) **...the fields of Jaar** (JAY-uhr) (Psalm 132:6): Ephrathah is believed to be a synonym for the area of Bethlehem (compare Micah 5:2), appropriately mentioned in a psalm about King David, one of the area's two most famous native sons. Some experts identify the fields of Jaar as a borderland between Judah and Benjamin.

• **King Sihon, of the Amorites, and King Og, of Bashan:** These kings make two cameos in today's readings (Psalm 135:11; 136:19-20). These monarchs were the first Canaanite kings that Israel conquered when taking possession of the Promised Land (see Numbers 21). So, as well as being literal figures, they symbolize the many enemies of God's people, the enemies whom God defeated for them.

4 Prayer

God, help me recall how your steadfast love endures forever. Thank you for your faithfulness. Amen.

75

Let It Be So!
Psalms 140–150

 Scouting the Terrain

People of faith want to pray "at all times" (Ephesians 6:18) and "without ceasing" (1 Thessalonians 5:17). We want to offer praise and

thanksgiving to God; we do not want to forget God in our good times. But part of the good news of our faith is that God is for us even in the bad times. Christians know this truth because God met us as one of us in Jesus Christ and lovingly chose to suffer as we do. "Cast all your anxiety on him," the apostle Peter tells us, "because he cares for you" (1 Peter 5:7).

The first half of today's readings find the psalm singers in some pretty desperate straits: plotted against by the wicked, endangered by their traps, fainting in spirit because of foes' oppression. We don't know all of the specifics; but we don't need to, because at some time, we have felt the same way. When we find ourselves in desperation, may we say, like the ancients, "But my eyes are turned toward you, O GOD, my Lord; in you I seek refuge; do not leave me defenseless" (Psalm 141:8).

• When have you prayed to God in a time of trouble? What happened?

• Do you think that God places more value on prayers offered under some circumstances differently from prayers offered under other circumstances? Why, or why not?

NOW READ PSALMS 140–150.

Road Signs

• **Hallelujah:** The Hebrew word that begins Psalms 146–150 literally means "Praise Yah[weh]" or "Praise the LORD," as many English translations indicate.

3 Switchback

The composer of Psalm 147 didn't have access to telescopes or computer-aided astronomy, but he or she wasn't trying to make a scientific statement when proclaiming that God "determines the number of the stars . . . [and] gives to all of them their names" (verse 4). No, the psalm singer is using poetic language to talk about the power and majesty of God. It is the language of doxology, the language of praise.

Psalms 146–150 bring both Book V and the entire psalter to a fitting finish: long and loud doxologies, songs of praise to God. These psalms remind us of what one Reformation-era catechism identifies as the "chief end," or main purpose, of human existence: to glorify God and to enjoy God forever.

• How will your life this day be a song of praise, a doxology, to God?

Several of this week's psalms were composed so that its singers would learn a lesson. Review all that you've read in Psalms 107–150, outlining lessons learned. Take an online quiz at amazingbiblerace.com to check your research.

4 Prayer

Lord, may my prayers ever praise you. Help me continually glorify and enjoy you. Amen.

Water Break

Congratulations! You've finished another book of the Bible. Allow the songs of God to cheer you on as you keep running.

Next, you'll be able to sprint quickly through Proverbs, picking up practical advice for everyday living. Take a deep breath and get ready to read some good stuff from a real "wise guy."

The Beginning of Wisdom
Proverbs 1

1 Scouting the Terrain

The Book of Proverbs opens with a father's calling his son to study and embrace wisdom. King Solomon is generally accepted as the author of Proverbs 1 and many other proverbs, although some scholars dispute his authorship. However, we can safely assume is that these bits of wisdom were used by King Solomon as a person, as a father, and as a king. A primary theme of Proverbs is stated in verse 7: "Fear of the LORD is the beginning of knowledge."

Trailblazer

• **Solomon**

Verse 8 begins the father's lesson about competing affections: his family's tradition of wisdom and the world's attractive folly. You will also notice that, in verses 20-33, "wisdom" is personified as a woman. This female personification of wisdom is one of the most consistent characterizations in the book.

• What sort of advice do you normally receive from your parent(s) and how does it compare with the parental advice from the passage?

• Do you consider yourself to be a wise person or a foolish one? Answer honestly. If you're not sure, just give it your best shot.

2 NOW READ PROVERBS 1.

Switchback

Decisions, decisions, decisions. Where do you turn for help in making life's toughest decisions? The Book of Proverbs is a great resource for learning more about the pursuit of wisdom. Verse 4 makes it clear that these proverbs are written to give "knowledge and prudence to the young."

The first concrete piece of advice that Proverbs offers us is concerned with the company we keep; that is, it forces us to ask the question, "Who are we hanging out with?" The parental figure warns us of the dangers of being in bad company. Verses 8-19 warn us that, if we spend time with people who draw us toward sin, we'll be changed for the worse. The writer tells us that the path of the sinner is death.

Wisdom herself speaks to those who have rejected her. Her message echoes that of the father.

• What's the benefit of seeking wisdom while you are still young?

• How would you describe the character of the people you hang out with?

Road Signs

• **garland** (1:9): This wreath of flowers or leaves indicates honor or praise.

4 Prayer

Lord, please give me a desire for wisdom. Help me wisely choose my friends, that I might encourage them as they encourage me. Tune my ear to the voice of wisdom over the next three weeks. Amen.

Can You Put Wisdom in a Bank?
Proverbs 2–3

1 Scouting the Terrain

The second chapter highlights the necessity of moral character development and demonstrates the benefits of making wise decisions and the dangers of making foolish ones. You may notice the use of the word *way,* which really means "way of life." So every time you see "way," just read it as "way of life" or "lifestyle." Embracing these wise ways leads to life (verses 20-22).

Trailblazer
• Solomon

Chapter 3 continues the father's instructions to ethical living, which pleases God. The father also offers direction for finding security and peace in God while dealing with those around you.

• What sort of "way" or lifestyle are you living?

• Why is upright moral character pleasing to God? Why would a pursuit of morality and ethics be included in these proverbs about seeking wisdom?

• Which do you desire more—material wealth, or wisdom? Which do you need more? Why?

2 NOW READ PROVERBS 2–3.

3 Switchback

These two chapters challenge us to seek a wise way of living. In ancient biblical times, people sought after silver and gold. Twenty-first century folks do the same thing, except our desires are for piles of cash, luxury sports cars, and designer clothes.

In Proverbs 3:13-18, we are told that wisdom is more valuable than silver and gold and more precious than jewels. While we could quickly rattle off the benefit of having thousands of dollars in the bank or driving a new car off the lot, the value of wisdom is not always apparent. Scripture tells us, however, that the person who possesses wisdom has peace, a long life, and more income and revenue than cherished material riches.

• If you could own the car of your choice or own wisdom, which would you choose? Why you would choose it?

• How difficult is it for you to see long life and peace as more attractive than having lots of money?

Racing Tip

The entire second chapter of Proverbs is an acrostic poem, with each verse beginning with one of the 22 letters of the Hebrew alphabet.

4 Prayer

Abundant God, help me trust you for my needs. Create in me a desire for wisdom above all earthly things. Amen.

Interview at least three adults connected with your team (a team member's parent, your youth leader, your Race Director, and so on). Ask them to talk about advice received from their parents. What rules or advice did they initially think were lame or ridiculous but later found full of wisdom? Make a video of your interviews in a creative way. Choose a talk show, a reality TV show, a newscast, or some other fun format to showcase your interviews. Have fun with it. Then upload your video to *amazingbiblerace.com* to earn points.

Grandpa Always Said . . .
Proverbs 4–5

1 Scouting the Terrain

Trailblazer

• Solomon

The lessons continue to the son from the father. Chapter four begins with the grandfather's lesson, which repeats the instruction to gain wisdom. Grandfather said that doing so produces protection and honor. God's people have long depended upon the transfer of information and instruction through the family generations. It's no surprise, then, that the father quotes his own father to validate his own advice-giving.

The chapter continues with instruction to stay away from the paths of the wicked (verses 10-19) and, once on the right way, to stay focused on it (verses 20-27). Chapter 5 addresses sexual sin, warning the son to stay away from another man's straying wife and to be devoted to his own wife (verses 1-23).

• What one story, tradition, or piece of advice has been handed down to you from a grandparent or other older relative? How is it an important piece of your family's identity?

• What would your life be like if you followed every piece of advice given by your parent(s) or other older family member(s)? What is it like for you to remember and follow your their advice?

2 NOW READ PROVERBS 4–5.

3 Switchback

Most of you reading this probably aren't married and are wondering how chapter 5 applies to you right now. Our society is one that is sex-saturated, with God's design of the marital covenant often being dismissed as some impossible ideal. Part of God's plan for God's people, though, is teaching the children about covenant marriage. It's never too early to begin thinking about what marital faithfulness really means in our culture.

Even though Proverbs was written for a patriarchial society and the intended audience was male, there's guidance here for both sexes. Taken at face value, today's Scripture points us to fidelity in marriage: Married men are to resist tempting women and remain devoted and faithful to their wives. Women are not to tempt married men. These lessons, though, can also be applied to temptations outside the sexual realm. Anything that replaces God as an affection of the heart leads to death. In our culture, sex is certainly a glaring temptation. Know that God created you a sexual being and designed your sexuality to be expressed within the proper covenantal relationship.

• What are the biggest sexual temptations you face?

• How could sexual activity now affect your future relationships?

4 Prayer

Merciful God, forgive me for straying from your wisdom, and help me seek your wisdom every day. Amen.

Listen Here, My Child . . .
Proverbs 6–7

1 Scouting the Terrain

We should not make promises we cannot keep. Chapter 6 begins with the command not to assume anyone else's debt. In today's lingo, that means that you should not cosign for a loan.

Trailblazer

• **Solomon**

Possessing a strong work ethic is next, as the father warns against laziness and commends diligence. He calls the son "lazybones," directing him to learn from the hard work of ants.

Next, we learn of the troublemaker. This individual is described in three ways: things about him or her that the Lord hates, a list of misused body parts, and antisocial behaviors.

• Did you ever make a promise to someone but didn't keep it? How did it feel to have this hanging over your head?

WEEK 8 ◆ DAY 4

• How would you describe your work ethic? How would your parents, boss, or teachers describe your work ethic?

• What are some things named in Chapter 6 that tempt you away from God?

2 NOW READ PROVERBS 6–7.

3 Switchback

Chapter 7 is another sex talk for the son. This time, the father uses graphic language to warn his son about the dangers of the "loose woman," "adulteress," or "prostitute." The father points out that temptation involves all of the senses. This adulteress uses linen, perfume, and seductive speech to lure the young man to her bed while her husband is away from home.

Try to apply this Scripture to your current circumstances. Temptations present themselves as beautiful and enticing. Often, our sense of sight is the first sense to be attracted to the temptation, which leads us to sin. For example, consider the first sin of humankind: Eve's sin was eating a piece of food that was "a delight to the eyes," (Genesis 3:6). When our eyes—as well as the rest of our senses—are focused on God, we successfully resist the appeal of temptation: "I will meditate on your precepts, and fix my eyes on your ways" (Psalm 119:15).

• When have you experienced God's working in you to reject some sort of temptation?

• Why, do you think, does the father once again speak with his son about sexual temptation?

Road Signs

• **"Apple of your eye"** (7:2): This phrase means that something or someone is the object of your deepest desires or that you care for most.

• **Myrrh, aloes, and cinnamon** (7:17): During biblical times, these perfumes were purchased only by kings and other wealthy people who traveled abroad. The woman was willing to use these expensive scents to satisfy her sexual passion. She argued that her indulgent invitation was an offer the young man could not refuse.

4 Prayer

Generous God, help me keep my promises, work hard, and keep my eyes fixed on you. Amen.

A Tale of Two Women
Proverbs 8–9

Scouting the Terrain

Once again, wisdom speaks. This time, she provides a balanced contrast to the adulteress from chapter 7. Wisdom is personified and given human characteristics and qualities. She has a mouth and a voice. She walks, was birthed, and is creative. She cooks a meal and prepares a banquet table (9:2).

Trailblazers
- **Wisdom**
- **Folly**

Wisdom's rival, folly, is also personified in chapter 9. Folly, too, has a voice. She sits and loudly calls to passersby.

Consider wisdom and folly. How are they similar? How are they different? Folly and adultering are similar. Both are loud and unruly. Both offer enticing invitations that ultimately lead to death. Folly targets those who seek to do right, "going straight on their way," (verse 15).

Both wisdom and folly call out. However, one offers virtuous insight; and the other offers destruction.

- How does the personification of wisdom and folly bring the truth of Scripture alive for you?

- When has wisdom called out to you? When has folly called out to you? How did you respond?

2. NOW READ PROVERBS 8–9.

3 Switchback

Almost everyone is interested in getting smarter, figuring out the best way to do something, or finding a fool-proof technique for effective decision-making. At first glance, you may be tempted to view Proverbs as a quick how-to guide for obtaining wisdom. After all, the father does a pretty good job listing the benefits of pursuing wisdom; and wisdom herself speaks convincingly of all of the great things she offers. We also receive a few lists of good and bad moral traits to provide a few concrete examples of wise living.

But read more closely. Wisdom reminds us that "the fear of the LORD is the beginning of wisdom, and the knowledge of the Holy One is insight" (9:10). While the lists are true of those who seek wisdom, acquisition of these traits do not alone make a person wise. True wisdom comes only from the fear of the Lord. Proverbs 8:17 implies that wisdom, like God, extends grace to those who seek her (compare with Isaiah 55:6). Jesus also uses this grace-centered seeking and finding imagery about himself in Matthew 7:7. It's easy to see, therefore, why some Bible scholars view wisdom in Proverbs as a foreshadow of Christ.

• Review the first nine chapters of Proverbs. Where do you see obvious similarities to Christ and his work?

• Read Proverbs 8:27-31 with Hebrews 1:1-2. What connections do you make between the two passages? Blog about what you've learned.

Water Break

Don't be discouraged if all this talk of Wisdom and Folly has your head spinning. Ask for the Holy Spirit's discernment. A deeper understanding will come as God makes all things clearer to you.

4 Prayer

God of wisdom, help me to listen to wisdom and to turn from folly. Amen.

Proverbs 8 is a balanced response to Proverbs 7. Study both chapters and the two women described there. With your team, list all the descriptions of the "loose woman" in chapter 7. Find the opposite descriptions of the wisdom, in chapter 8. Once your lists are complete, take a quiz online at *amazingbiblerace.com* for points.

If A, Then B
Proverbs 10–12

1 Scouting the Terrain

Chapter 10 takes a sharp turn in style from the previous chapters, featuring a series of two-liners. These lines are parallel, with contrasting meaning. The message of these lines is that the morally righteous are wise. Each statement carries a set of promised outcomes of righteous behavior (or its opposite). Solomon's sayings touch on a variety of aspects of everyday life: wealth, speech, security, and deeds. At first glance, we may assume that these are pieces of advice similar to fortune cookie sayings or bumper sticker quotations. But remember that they comprise Scripture and have far deeper application for one's life. Yes, they are good advice for living; but they also possess the key to life.

Trailblazer
• Solomon

• When have you made a wise decision that resulted in a good outcome?

• How do your actions directly affect events in your life? When has a negative result come from your foolish action?

2 NOW READ PROVERBS 10–12.

3 Switchback

The Proverbs give sound advice for everyday life. The special gift of God's Word, though, is its deeper meaning that comes alive when viewed from an eternal perspective.

Proverbs 10:2 says, "Treasures gained by wickedness do not profit." Common sense and experience tell us that any possession or achievement is most satisfying when we work hard for it, not when we steal it or acquire it in some other dishonest way. Because we live in a fallen world; however, these principles do not always play out according to fairness and truth. Instead, as believers, we can see that the righteous way is a glimpse—a foretaste— of the outcomes for the righteous for eternity. In this case, our treasures gained by righteousness are the most rewarding of all: new life in Christ.

- When have you pursued something in a righteous manner and obtained it? How did this feel?

- When have you pursued something in a righteous manner but did not obtain it? How did this feel?

- Which is worth more to you—earthly possessions and achievements or eternal life? How is your answer demonstrated in your life right now?

4 Prayer

Gracious God, forgive me for desiring earthly treasures. Give me a longing for eternity with you. Amen.

Proverbs

Bite Your Tongue!
Proverbs 13–15

1 Scouting the Terrain

If you think that Chapter 13 sounds like something you've already read, it's because the author, Solomon, continues the two-line sayings and revisits some familiar themes: speech, wealth and ethics, satisfied longings, and eternity.

Chapter 14 speaks of what it means to walk in wisdom and not to live by appearances. Verse 4 conveys a key theme: Wealth increases due to

Trailblazer

• Solomon

hard work. The way one handles his or her circumstances is addressed in verses 13-19, while the chapter ends with a contrast of the righteous and the wicked.

Solomon highlights the importance of gentle speech and instruction in 14:33-15:4. He teaches the importance of upholding righteousness with a gentle tongue. Painful words have painful consequences, while gentle words mend damage.

• When have your words hurt someone? When have they helped someone?

• Why, do you think, does speech have such an effect on us?

• Has your tongue ever been "deceitful" (15:4, NIV)? What happened to your spirit and/or to another's spirit?

2 NOW READ PROVERBS 13–15.

③ Switchback

Have you had a bad day? a bad week? a bad couple of months? What happened? We all go through periods of being down, having pity parties. Sometimes, we experience dark valleys of depression and face difficult struggles.

Proverbs 15 speaks to the ability of the heart to triumph over circumstances. Have you ever known someone who was facing a serious illness, was going through financial hardship, or had lost a loved one; yet he or she praised God?

Beginning in verse 13, Solomon writes of the difference between a happy heart and a sorrowful heart. He shows us the experiences of those who live in wisdom (happy heart) or folly (sorrowful heart). According to Solomon, the way you deal with life's circumstances really is a choice, which begins with choosing wisdom (the fear of the Lord, in verse 16).

• When have you experienced a happy heart in spite of difficult circumstances?

Road Signs

• **Abaddon** (15:11): In Hebrew, *Abaddon* means "destruction." In this verse, it points to a place of destruction in conjunction with Sheol (the place of the dead).

Weekly Challenge

Proverbs 13 uses the metaphor of eating food to convey the idea that morally upright teaching and living produces good things. With your team, make a list of all the images of eating (and the intended message) in Proverbs 13. Take a quiz at *amazingbiblerace.com* to see how well your search went.

④ Prayer

God of mercy, give me wisdom and a happy heart. Amen.

Step by Step
Proverbs 16–18

WEEK
9
◇
DAY
3

1 Scouting the Terrain

The next seven chapters are often referred to as the "royal collection" because they explore social roles and structures in a royal life setting. In part, these proverbs were used in the royal courts to teach young people how they should function within their society and grow to rule with wisdom. As you read, try to imagine yourself as an adolescent in the time of King Solomon.

Trailblazer
• **Solomon**

Many of the verses contrast the plans of human beings with the plans of God. The goal is to help young people realize that, above all, God is in control. Your success is entirely dependent on God's divine direction. Another prominent theme is controlling the tongue. If you haven't figured it out by now, wisdom is closely connected with keeping a tight rein on your words.

• Have you ever made a plan to do something that just seemed to fail miserably? Why, do you think, did it fail?

• Do you believe that God ultimately directs all things? Why, or why not?

2 NOW READ PROVERBS 16–18.

③ Switchback

In 16:3 we are told to commit all of our work to the Lord. When we do so, our plans, work, and outcome will succeed. Verse 9 says that, even though we make plans for all of the things we want to accomplish, God ultimately orders and directs our steps. In verse 18, Solomon tells us that destruction comes from pride. This type of "pride" is the notion that any good result or blessing comes from outside God's hands. Human pride says, "I did this all on my own." This strips God of the glory in directing our steps. This is why those who fail to acknowledge that all good things come from God will ultimately face destruction.

The issue of controlling our tongues is also heavily present in this passage. These verses tells us that "righteous lips" are pleasing to the king (16:13), pleasant words are like a "honeycomb" (16:24), that even fools who say nothing will appear wise (17:28), and that the tongue possesses the power of both life and death (18:21). Many other verses portray the positive effects of controlling our tongues and the negative results of coarse or hurtful words.

• What is the best way to ensure that God is directing your steps?

• What's the relationship between your plans and the Lord's directing your steps (see verse 9)?

④ Prayer

Sovereign God, I pray that my plans are your plans. Direct my steps every day. Amen.

Proverbs

Words to Live By
Proverbs 19–21

WEEK
9
◆
DAY
4

1 Scouting the Terrain

A close reading of chapter 19 reveals a list of fools. Laziness, wickedness, violence, drunkenness are all represented here as foolish behavior. Verse 23 tells us about the wise one, while verse 24 contrasts the lifestyle of the wise by describing the habits of a lazy person. Next we read of shameful children who do violence to their father and chase away their mother, corrupt witnesses who destroy social order, and the brawling drunkard who has been led astray by wine and threatens those around him or her.

Trailblazer

• Solomon

Chapter 20 is a sobering picture of the righteous king cleansing his kingdom of these fools. Verse 2 speaks of a king's anger being like "the growling of a lion." The king's subjects have turned from wisdom to folly and have provoked the king. Verse 8 speaks of the king's righteous judgment. The winnowing in verses 8 and 26 paints the picture of the king sorting through and weeding out the wicked from the righteous.

The king of the Book of Proverbs foreshadows the King of Kings. God's righteous judgment is also full of mercy. God does not judge the wicked based upon their actions. Their actions are indicative only of the state of their hearts. Those who grasp wisdom will not act foolishly but righteously.

• Read Matthew 25:31-46 and Proverbs 19:23-20:11. Who are the sheep? Who are the goats? How are the two passages related? Are you a sheep or a goat?

2 NOW READ PROVERBS 19–21.

③ Switchback

Verse 19:17 tells us that "whoever is kind to the poor, lends to the Lord, and will be repaid in full." When you are kind to the poor, what are you lending to God? You lend your time, your prayers, your love, your material goods. The Scripture promises that in giving of yourself and your means, you will be repaid in full. Serving the poor is an act of sacrificial worship. Romans 12:1 says, "... present your bodies as a living sacrifice, holy and acceptable to God, which is your spiritual worship."

In 21:13 we learn that those who ignore the poor will not be heard in their time of desperation. This verse does not advocate superficial compassion simply for the guarantee that God will treat you well. Solomon points out that the foolish person (who is not motivated by mercy) will be judged without mercy (see James 2:13).

- How much do you notice the needs of the poor around you? What could you do to increase your awareness?

- Why is it good to have compassion on the poor?

Road Signs

- **Surety** (20:16): This is the condition of being sure beyond doubt, a certainty.

Proverbs

Winnowing is the process by which chaff is separated and removed from grain. Today, mechanical combines do the job.

With your team, visit a modern-day farm that uses a combine for harvesting grain. Ask the farmer to explain the process to you. Also ask the farmer to comment on his or her understanding of winnowing, as mentioned in the Bible.

Take a video of your trip to the farm and your interview with the farmer. Be creative with the finished product and upload it to *amazingbiblerace.com* for points.

④ Prayer

Loving God, help me care for those who need to feel your love. Amen.

Words of the Wise
Proverbs 22–24

1 Scouting the Terrain

Today's section of Proverbs finishes off the "royal court" wisdom and moves into a section that is thought have been inserted into this part of the book. Proverbs 22:1-16 reminds us of the reason that young people are a desired audience for wisdom literature. Verse 22:6 commands parents to commit their child rearing to a wise course of action. The promise is that when they are older, they will fall back on that instruction. Verse 15 indicates that young people need this type of teaching because "folly is bound up" in the hearts of youth. Instruction and discipline are meant to act as guides to wise living, and the Scripture recognizes that each person is responsible for himself or herself before God.

Trailblazer
• Solomon

The next section of Proverbs is often called "Words of the Wise" as illustrated in Proverbs 22:17. Many scholars presume that it was not directly connected to the preceding proverbial sayings. In fact, it displays distinctive similarities to a piece of Egyptian wisdom literature called the "Instruction of Amenemope." This wisdom literature is from the period of the Ramses kings around 1100 B.C. The difference is, however, "Instruction of Amenemope" has 30 sections from which it guides the young person, whereas the "Words of the Wise" contains more than 30 sections.

• How have your parents, teachers, and church leaders trained you in the right way?

2 NOW READ PROVERBS 22–24.

③ Switchback

Often when we're young, we use appearance, grades, athletic ability, and clothing to measure our worth compared with our peers. As one gets older, possessing lots of money (and the things it can buy) becomes the ultimate point of comparison.

Solomon's proverbs have a lot to say about the uselessness of money when compared to the wisdom of God. Solomon is a credible authority on the topic, too, because he was the most wise and the most wealthy king to have ever lived (see 1 Kings 10:23). Solomon had everything he wanted—literally.

Chapter 22:29–23:8 focuses on greed. Food and money are not as they appear. A meal offered insincerely is not a gesture of friendship. Possessing great wealth does not give one security. Often those things that appear to offer a more satisfying life actually contain aspects that hinder and distract us from true satisfaction, found only in the wisdom of God.

• How do *you* measure someone's worth?

• How important are possessions to you? What satisfaction do you get from your possessions?

Water Break

You are running a great race so far. Congratulations for making it more than halfway through Proverbs. More wise sayings are ahead from Solomon, so take a break and get your thinking cap ready. Don't stop now!

④ Prayer

God of wisdom, help me not to desire the things of this world but to seek after your truth. Amen.

One of These Things Is not Like the Other
Proverbs 25–26

Scouting the Terrain

King Solomon is credited as the author of the next three chapters (two of which you will read today), but the officials of King Hezekiah of Judah are credited with copying and compiling them. Hezekiah became king after his father, Ahaz, died. His reign extended from the late 8th century to the early 7th century B.C. He was considered one of the good kings of Israel, because he reinstituted worship of the Israelite's God after a long period of idol worship.

Today's wisdom sayings demonstrate similarities in dissimilar things. They show how two different things can have a quality in common. The sayings use a lot of time-, season-, and nature-oriented imagery to teach acceptable social behaviors. These proverbs are similar to the royal court proverbs but were, perhaps, aimed at a broader audience.

- How you deal with other people's foolishness and poor decisions? Do you discourage or encourage it?

Trailblazers

- **Solomon**
- **Officials of King Hezekiah's court**

2. NOW READ PROVERBS 25–26.

3 Switchback

In Proverbs 26, verses 4 and 5 seem to offer contradictory advice. Verse 4 says that we shouldn't respond to someone's poor decision in a similar manner, because then we'll also be guilty of the same mistake. While verse 5 says that we should respond to someone's poor decision in the same way; otherwise the other person will think that he or she is doing the right thing.

Still confused? Remember that this proverb is showing similarities in dissimilar things. The similarity is the response of doing the same thing or acting in the same way as the foolish person.

The difference lies in the time, occasion, and motivation for our response. By placing the two contradictory statements together, the writer emphasizes that the goal is discernment for applying the proper response to the situation. In the end, each verse is its own separate proverb, but both are connected by responding to the fool in the same way. Each verse addresses two different situations; the response would depend on the particular situation.

• Next time you encounter someone making a foolish decision, how might you respond (based on what you have just read)?

• Describe two different situations that might illustrate Proverbs 26:4-5.

4 Prayer

God of discernment, help me be wise in all my interactions with others so that I might know how to respond to others with their best interests in mind. Amen.

Who's Got Your Back?
Proverbs 27

Scouting the Terrain

Of the many themes in Proverbs 27, a couple stand out as particularly useful for modern-day young people. Unfortunately, we live in a society that is obsessed with image. We are constantly concerned with what others think about us. The chapter addresses how we should see ourselves and those factors that contribute to how others might see us. It is concerned with how we appear to others in what we say and do. We often try to puff ourselves up to make ourselves feel better. This chapter seeks to address those self-perception issues.

Trailblazer

• **Solomon**

• Make a note of all of the verses that speak to the themes of self-perception and others' perception of you. Write down key words from the verses.

• Think of a time when you bragged about yourself recently. How did it make you feel after you praised yourself?

• Do you ever praise or encourage others? Why, or why not?

NOW READ PROVERBS 27.

③ Switchback

In a society that tempts us to isolate ourselves with technological advances, today's passage reminds us of the benefits of human relationships. Could Solomon have imagined a world full of Internet connections, e-mail, and text messaging? Probably not. (But then again, he was the wisest person to have ever lived, so maybe so.) Regardless, cultivating close personal relationships goes beyond IM-ing with someone in a chatroom.

Verse 8 speaks of the hurt associated with not having roots. One who wanders hurts both himself or herself and those to whom he or she is connected. Verse 10 points out that one should develop friendships beyond family ties because sometimes family members are unwilling or unable to assist in a time of need. Verse 17 says that iron sharpens iron. Interacting with others produces a positive outcome in our own character.

- Think of all of the relationships in your life. Which give you roots? To what friends do you turn in times of need? Which of those relationships sharpens your own character?

④ Prayer

God of love, help me encourage those around me and not seek praise for myself. Amen.

As a team, start a new relationship-building ministry. Who needs encouragement? Here are some idea starters:

- **Big Buddy:** Pair older youth or young adults with younger kids who live in single-parent homes.
- **Adopt-a-Grandparent:** Pair youth with persons at a nursing home or retirement home.
- **After-School:** Have activities (games, snacks, tutoring, Bible study) for kids at your church.
- **Prayer Partners:** Pair youth with older adults, with youth in your large group, or with youth from another church's youth group.

To get points, post on *amazingbiblerace.com* a video blog or photos of your team creating and participating in the ministry. You must also upload a scan of a covenant signed by each team member to commit to this ministry for at least three months.

Flipping the Script
Proverbs 28–29

1 Scouting the Terrain

In this section, we find the writer addressing those who are wicked and greedy. It is written in a similar style as the previous wisdom sayings. By this time in your study of Proverbs, you should see a lot of recurring themes in these two chapters. While this section offers general instruction for the reader, it addresses the theme of greediness, with a greater emphasis than in many of the previous chapters.

• Do you think that greed is a problem in our country? Where do you see greed the most?

Trailblazers

• **Solomon**
• **Officials of King Hezekiah's court**

• Have you been greedy or selfish lately? How?

• Think of a particular time when you were generous toward others. How did that make you feel?

2 NOW READ PROVERBS 28–29.

3 Switchback

These two chapters contrast greediness with our trust in the Lord. In 28:25, we find that greedy people cause many problems because they are looking out only for themselves. The writer tells us that, rather than watching out for number one, when we trust in God to supply all our needs, we will be enriched. It is wise to trust in God's provision, and it is foolish to rely on only our own means for reward. In verse 27, we are challenged not only to rid ourselves from greed but to give freely to others who are less fortunate than we. It's the ultimate reversal. If we give, we will receive. On the other hand, it also tells us that if we are too greedy to meet the needs of the poor and we ignore them, we will be cursed. Again, the theme of "you reap what you sow" is used.

Because we are inclined to self-preservation and are generally prone to greed, we are challenged to live a generous lifestyle. Christ, the Ultimate Giver, is not only a model of the way we should live. His perfect life, death, and resurrection enables us to live as he commands. Through Christ, we can be selfless, giving, and generous.

Proverbs

• How can you act differently when greedy impulses spring up in you?

• In what ways, other than with money, could and does God bless those who are generous?

Proverbs 28 has much to say about handling money. Read verses 6, 8, 20, 22, 25, and 27. Circle the words *poor, rich, wealth, greedy*. What is the message of these verses? Now read 1 Timothy 6:6-10. How does the New Testament passage help you understand the Proverbs verses? Go to *amazingbiblerace.com* and take a quiz to show what you've learned.

4 Prayer

Generous God, help me not to be greedy but to give freely from all of the blessings you have given me. Amen.

Us Compared to God
Proverbs 30

1 Scouting the Terrain

The next two chapters might seem somewhat disconnected from the first 29 chapters of the book. First, they are credited to other sources outside of Solomon's house and the royal court. Chapter 30, your reading for today, is credited to Agur, the son of Jakeh. There is much scholarly debate over Agur's identity. Was he simply the compiler of these wise sayings, or did he play a more significant role? For our purposes, however, it is enough to recognize that these sayings didn't come directly from Solomon, despite the overlap in a lot of the instruction. One interesting literary feature of this chapter is its use of numbers and lists in poetic imagery. In many verses, it is almost as though we are given riddles through which we must find the instruction.

Trailblazer

• Agur

Another unique emphasis in this chapter is found in the first five verses. You will find an acknowledgement of failure to attain wisdom. It's ironic because it comes after 29 chapters of instruction on how to be wise. Perhaps this is a case of "the more you know, the more you realize how much you don't really know." The meaning of the writer's claim to have learned no wisdom is described in verse 4. He is acutely aware that he can never truly understand God.

• What does it mean to demonstrate wisdom?

2 NOW READ PROVERBS 30.

3 Switchback

We live in an information-saturated society, where answers are only as far away as our computers and smart phones. With the Internet and twenty-four-hour news channels streaming countless bits of information to us each day, it's a wonder why, as a culture, we are not wiser. Perhaps this is because human knowledge and godly wisdom are not the same thing.

Think about how many usernames, passwords, phone numbers, and song lyrics you have running around in your brain at this exact moment. Some researchers say that many teenagers today have more information running around in their heads than Albert Einstein ever did.

After the twenty-nine chapters of wisdom literature, it is not by chance that the thirtieth reminds us of our limitedness in human wisdom. This chapter reminds us of the fallibility of humanity and the infinite wisdom of God. Wisdom is a process. The first step toward God's wisdom is knowing that being wise is not an end at which to arrive but a journey on which we grow. God's wisdom comes only from God.

• How, do you think, does this chapter tie in with the rest of the Book of Proverbs?

• What are the biggest obstacles to becoming a wise person?

4 Prayer

God of wisdom, I ask for your wisdom, according to your Word. Amen.

You Go, Girl!
Proverbs 31

1 Scouting the Terrain

The closing chapter of Proverbs has two parts where women figure prominently. King Lemuel is credited with being the author of chapter 31.

Trailblazer
• King Lemuel

Some scholars, however, consider King Lemuel to be a pseudonym (alternative name) for King Solomon, because there is no record of a King Lemuel in Israelite history.

Verses 1 through 9 are instructions from King Lemuel's mother about how to best meet the needs of the afflicted, whereas verses 10 through 31 offer us an ode to a capable wife in the form of an acrostic poem. (Each verse starts with one of the 22 letters of the Hebrew alphabet.)

• How, do you think, should a ruler of a country govern his or her people?

• What does it mean to be a "capable wife"?

• Why are the characteristics of a "capable wife" traits toward which we should all aspire?

WEEK
10
◇
DAY
5

2 NOW READ PROVERBS 31.

3 Switchback

The first part of this chapter deals with two warnings: 1) Don't be ruled by fleshly desires, and 2) don't allow alcohol to alter your judgment. These warnings remind us that giving in to these two temptations can cloud our ability to make decisions, causing us to forget the needs of the afflicted in the world. Clear thought enables us to meet the needs of those who are poor and oppressed. We are also encouraged to speak out for those whose voices are not heard.

In verses 10-31 of the acrostic poem, we find the humanized counterpart of Wisdom from Proverbs 8. The capable wife is a woman full of virtuous qualities, including trust (verses 11-12); industry, initiative, and imagination (verses 13-19); compassion (v. 20); provision (verses 21-25); and wisdom (verse 26).

Whew! Do you know anyone—man or woman—who simultaneously embodies all of these traits? While Wisdom's female human representation is the Proverbs 31 wife (Wisdom's New Testament fulfillment is Christ himself), we should realize that no human could ever live up this standard of perfection. We are reminded that all of these attributes are produced from a heart changed by God. The book ends as it began (Proverbs 1:7): The beginning of wisdom is the fear of God (verse 30).

• Which qualities of the capable wife do you see in yourself? How might you pray for the Holy Spirit to enable you to live as the capable wife is described?

Water Break

Congratulations, you've completed another book of the Bible! Here's a daily devotion idea to take with you: Consider that Proverbs is 31 chapters long. Read one chapter of Proverbs each day. Whatever day of the month it is, read that chapter. Yeah, we know that chapter 31 will occasionally get cut off; but overall, the years of reading this wisdom book will pay off. That's a promise.

4 Prayer

Gracious God, help me fear you so that I may become wise. Amen.

All for Nothing
Ecclesiastes 1–2

 Scouting the Terrain

Ecclesiastes begins with a connection to King Solomon through a relational reference (son of David, king of Jerusalem). But the book's author, Qohelet (koh-HEL-ith), which is translated as "the Teacher," does not claim to be King Solomon, nor does he even mention Solomon by name.

Trailblazer

• Qohelet (the Teacher)

Scholars disagree as to who the true author is. Regardless, the author assumes a Solomon-like persona (if it's not Solomon himself) in order to convey credibility for his writings.

The vanity of life echoes throughout the book. The Teacher begins with this assertion. The Hebrew word for *vanity* means "breath" or "vapor." He implies that life is useless, meaningless, fleeting, and futile.

Chapter 2 continues the observations of meaninglessness as the Teacher points out earthly pleasures. We learn that he has literally everything but describes it all as mere vanity.

• What gives meaning to life? What is the purpose of life?

2. NOW READ ECCLESIASTES 1–2.

③ Switchback

Some Bible students find Ecclesiastes depressing. The Teacher sounds so negative about everything. The Teacher's main point (which will continue to be revealed) is that human efforts can do nothing to affect the eternal realm of our beings. He claims that the pleasures we receive on earth from our toils are our rewards. In this way, life is vanity for Qohelet. It's just a twinkling in the eye of the earth. One moment it's here and the next moment it's not!

Road Signs

- **"delights of the flesh, and many concubines"** (2:8): The meaning of the Hebrew word for *concubine* in this sense is uncertain. Given the context of this verse, however, it was likely to have been associated with sexuality and sexual activity. At the time of this writing, having multiple wives and mistresses was socially acceptable.

In the middle of all this, though, is a glimmer of hope. In verse 24, the writer credits God with goodness and pleasure. The Teacher reminds us that our sovereign God is the giver of good gifts.

- How do you view the work you do on earth? How do you understand the pleasures of hard work while also acknowledging their fleeting nature?

hurdle It's easy to get lost in Ecclesiastes. The writer says that all we do in life—apart from fear God—is vanity (or meaningless). We've posted a list for you at *amazingbiblerace.com* to help you keep track of the writer's points made throughout the book.

④ Prayer

Gracious God, help me remember that all blessings come from your hands. Amen.

Seasons
Ecclesiastes 3–4

Scouting the Terrain

A popular song from the 1960s owes its inspiration to Ecclesiastes 3. The Byrds' "Turn! Turn! Turn!" (a.k.a. "To Everything There Is a Season") was a hit song that your parents and grandparents likely remember. You may have even heard it yourself, since it has been used in commercials, television shows, and in the movie *Forrest Gump*.

The first eight verses of Ecclesiastes 3 contain fourteen comparative seasons of life. Verse 9 through the end of chapter 3 look to God as the cause of all things. Qohelet continues in the same language that he uses in the first eight verses and in the general theme of enjoying the fruits of one's labors. The new element added to this mix, however, is a direct reference to God's judgment. Qohelet makes it clear that judgment comes from the hand of God.

Trailblazer

• **Qohelet (the Teacher)**

Chapter 4 addresses the relationships between humans. It looks at the oppressed and the oppressor, the dead and the living, the lazy and those who toil, those without friends and those who stand in solidarity, and a young person and the king. As you read the next two chapters, see whether you can insert yourself in one of these comparisons.

• Describe a hard time in your life that seemed to last forever. How can you look at that time now as only a "season"?

NOW READ ECCLESIASTES 3–4.

3 Switchback

Life can be hard. Maybe you've had a fight with your parents. Maybe you are struggling with a severe or fatal illness. Are you falling behind in school? Did you not make the cut for a sports team?

Maybe things are going well for you. You're on top of the world, enjoying smooth relationships, great grades, and membership in all the teams and clubs you've gone out for.

Ecclesiastes reminds us that life is not static. To every purpose, there is a season. Life will not stay the same. So if you find yourself in a valley, be encouraged that a mountain peak is ahead. If you are on top today, prepare your heart for tough times that will inevitably come.

Know that God is with us through all of the ups and downs. Although our circumstances change, our God does not. Qohelet tells us that we cannot understand why we have these different seasons, just as we will never be able to truly understand the ways of God outside of that which God reveals to us in Scripture. Nonetheless, we are expected to trust in God's master plan for the world.

• How might you encourage a friend or family member who is going through a hard or difficult time?

Search the Scriptures for references to time. As you will discover, the biblical concept of time does not simply refer to the reading on your digital watch. Read these verses to learn more: **Genesis 18:14; Esther 4:14; Psalm 31:15; Ecclesiastes 8:5-6; and Acts 17:26.** Take a quiz at *amazingbiblerace.com* to show what you've learned.

4 Prayer

Sovereign God, I praise you for all of the seasons of my life. Amen.

What Really Matters
Ecclesiastes 5–6

1 Scouting the Terrain

In the first part of chapter 5, we find instruction on our interaction with and conception of God. Qohelet makes a stark distinction between God and humanity in this chapter, as he does in the book as a whole. He also warns us of the pointlessness of money and riches. He tells us that those who love money will never be satisfied and that there are greater riches on this earth than material wealth (for example, children [see 6:3]).

Trailblazer

- Qohelet (the Teacher)

Resist the temptation to moan, "What's the point of living, then?" as you continue through the Book of Ecclesiastes. Instead, concede that life on earth is temporary, while eternal things come through God. In the end, our hope comes from knowing that our sovereign God is in control.

- What promises have you made to God? How seriously do you take your church's membership vows?

- Do you love the idea of having a lot of money? Why? What good and/or bad things could result from having a lot of money?

2 NOW READ ECCLESIASTES 5–6.

3 Switchback

Road Signs

• **surfeit** (5:12): This word means "overindulgence," "excess," or "gluttony."

Have you ever said, "God, if you just help me out on this test, I promise that I will go to church every week without fighting with Mom about it." If you didn't utter that exact promise, you've probably said something similar. Chapter 5 tells us we shouldn't make promises to God that we cannot fulfill. In the Gospel of Matthew it says that we should let our yes be yes and our no be no. In other words, we should stand by our words, especially when talking to our Creator.

Qohelet tells us that even money—that which we use to buy earthly items—is temporary. It won't last. The book tells us not to store up our money but to enjoy it in this life, because we can't take it with us. We are not to seek after money so that we can have riches, but we are to enjoy life with those we love. Don't allow greed and selfishness to infest your life; but, rather, enjoy those blessings that come from God.

• How can you begin enjoying the blessings of your work, while not longing after money and the material goods of this world?

4 Prayer

God of all things, forgive me for promises that I have not kept and thank you for your eternal promises. Amen.

Ecclesiastes

You Can't Take It With You
Ecclesiastes 7–9

1 Scouting the Terrain

Once again, Qohelet says that there is no enduring good. He pairs opposites to show that one cannot exist without the other (joy and sorrow,

Trailblazer

• **Qohelet (the Teacher)**

verses 2 and 3, for example). Verses 13 and 14 remind us that God is the agent of the those life events that we cannot explain. Humans are to respond to circumstances as they occur. Our hope lies in our good God, who will ultimately bring good things to pass, despite our limited human experience.

Chapter 8 continues to address the elusive nature of wisdom, but with with royal imagery. Qohelet turns again to the unfathomable ways of God and our need for the fear of God before he extols the benefits of living life at its fullest. His basic message is this: All things are under God and we can enjoy those blessings that come from our earthly labor.

• Have you ever felt that those who do sinful things in this world are rewarded and those who to the righteous thing are punished? Why, do you think, does that sometimes happen?

2 NOW READ ECCLESIASTES 7–9.

3 Switchback

Ecclesiastes is like an old man looking back on life right before he dies (remember the old guy on the mountain top?). Qohelet has seen it all, done it all, and had it all. Truly, he has experienced all earthly pleasures and found no lasting return. Furthermore, he questions living righteously. He sees injustice and unfairness in his world. He sees the end for the wicked and the righteous as being the same: death.

We can glean a few things from this book. First, anything a person possesses will not ultimately satisfy. The created will not last. Only the things of God will endure. Second, despite those things we don't understand, God is in control. Sometimes that is the only truth that gives us comfort and joy. We don't have all of the answers, and we never will. Third, God's gifts are to be enjoyed. Just because we know that earthly gifts are mere shadows of the ultimate good gift of eternal life, that doesn't mean that we are to reject them. We know that flowers are beautiful because God is beautiful. Food is satisfying because God is satisfying. Relationships are heartwarming because God is heartwarming. If a loved one gives us a lovely piece of jewelry, we would wear it joyfully. We would enjoy it and be reminded of the giver. We would never give it back, saying, "No, thank you. This won't last forever or stay pretty forever, or it may break. I don't want your gift." So it is with God's gifts: They are to be enjoyed with gratitude in this life.

• What gifts has God given to you?

4 Prayer

Sovereign God, your wisdom is so great. Yet you call us to seek after wisdom and righteousness. Help me long for wisdom and righteousness, that I might be more like you. Amen.

115

Changes of Perspective
Ecclesiastes 10–12

1 Scouting the Terrain

In the last three chapter of Ecclesiastes, Qohelet reinforces the themes that have been presented in the book so far. Chapter 10 warns us that, because a little folly can hurt the wise, folly can affect the foolish even more. Still, we are reminded that the foolish sometimes do well for themselves. Qohelet goes on to point out that foolishness always results in ruin.

Trailblazer

• **Qohelet (the Teacher)**

In chapter 11, we find instructions for living diligently. To live diligently, be thoughtful and invest your life wisely.

Finally, in the second half of chapter 11 and in the eight verses of chapter 12, Qohelet compares the life of the young person with that of the old. He is quick to remind us that life is like the wind; and he urges us to enjoy life before it's too late, before the possibility of joy is gone.

• What is the difference between enjoying God's good gifts and living recklessly—pursuing enjoyment in things that are not good for you (underage drinking, sexual relationships, unhealthful eating habits, and so on)?

WEEK
11
◆
DAY
5

• Where is your focus: enjoying God's gifts now or always looking for the next thing that will make you happy (getting the right boyfriend/girlfriend/date, choosing the right college/career, and so on)?

2 NOW READ ECCLESIASTES 10–12.

Switchback

In verse 11:9, Qohelet tells us to rejoice in our youth and to follow the inclinations of our hearts and the desires of our eyes. Wait a second! Is this a license for having fun?

Not exactly. Qohelet gives us a very poignant "but!" He reminds us that everything we do and say will be judged by God someday. We will be held accountable for our actions and deeds.

While some of our blessings will come in this lifetime, we will have to answer for all choices we make on earth. The wisdom books beckon you to love the joys of life but to keep an eye on eternity. You are to fear God, because doing so is the beginning of wisdom. Although life is short, eternity isn't. Live for eternity!

All of wisdom literature is summed up in 12:13: "Fear God, and keep his commandments; for that is the whole duty of everyone." Doing so brings ultimate fulfillment.

• Describe your perspective on life. Is it eternal or earthly?

Water Break

We hope that Ecclesiastes didn't put you in a funk. (It has that effect on some readers.) Even though you may want to throw up your hands and shout back at Qohelet, "Hey, dude, what's the point?" don't! Ask the Holy Spirit to speak to you and teach you the hope of Ecclesiastes.

Get ready to change gears. Better than any big-screen "chick flick," the Song of Solomon is a tender love story, with embedded lessons about God's love for God's people.

Yeah, yeah, yeah, it's all a little syrupy. But don't stop now, with only one week to go in this leg. You're doing a great job reading your way through the best book ever written!

 Prayer

God of Wisdom, help me keep your commandments. Help me fear you. Give me wisdom. Amen.

Is It Just Infatuation?
Song of Solomon 1–2

 Scouting the Terrain

Today's reading offers us three poems. While the first verse attributes this book to Solomon, not all scholars agree that he was the author.

Trailblazers

- **The Bride (the Shulammite)**
- **The Bridegroom (the Beloved)**
- **The Friends (the daughters of Jerusalem)**

Many interpreters regard the book as an allegory for God's love for God's people. The story of the two lovers in the Song of Solomon reveals three aspects of love. The couple demonstrates desire, commitment, and giving of self. God, too, demonstrates these traits in God's love for us.

The Song is written in verse, as love poetry. All those English literature lessons will come in handy as you read this book. The Song is full of sensual imagery, metaphors, and allegories. Note the use of fruit, plant life, and landscape to describe the two lovers. It is highly emotional—both in the ideas it describes and the feelings elicited in the reader.

- What is the significance of God's using the story of the two lovers as a picture for God's love for you?

- How does the Song of Solomon affect the way you view covenant marriage?

2

**NOW READ
SONG OF SOLOMON 1–2.**

③ Switchback

In our society, a genuine reciprocal and mutual love is difficult to find. What popular culture attempts to call "love" more often falls under the category of infatuation or lust. The mass media is quick to redefine *love,* with the true biblical picture of faithful love shoved into the background.

The lovers in Song of Solomon, however, demonstrate an intense reciprocal love. The deep belonging portrayed in this book challenges us to consider our own belonging to Christ. In John 15, Jesus talks about abiding in him. This sort of *abiding* also means "remaining" or "dwelling." Does our love for Christ cause us to desire to dwell and remain with Christ? Are we able to say that Christ is ours and that we are Christ's? When we truly love Christ, we long to remain with him; that is, we long for his presence deep within our soul. Imagine the depth of your relationship with God when you deeply and intensely long for divine intimacy.

- What spiritual practices may increase your longing for Christ's presence in your life?

Road Signs

- **Kedar** (1:5): They were a desert tribe whose tents were made out of dark goat hair.
- **nard** (1:12): This expensive aromatic ointment was used as a perfume.
- **Engedi** (1:14): This city was a lush oasis on the west coast of the Dead Sea.

Song of Solomon

 The Song of Solomon is just one example in Scripture where the bridegroom's love for his bride (and their relationship) is an allegory of God's love for God's people. Read Isaiah 54:5-10; Jeremiah 2:2; and Hosea 2:14-20 to find similar comparisons. Then take a quiz at *amazingbiblerace.com* to show how much you've learned.

 ### ④ Prayer

Loving God, help me remain in your Spirit so that my longing for your presence might grow. Amen.

119

Dream a Little Dream
Song of Solomon 3

① Scouting the Terrain

The girl is not yet with her lover, but chapter 3 begins with her imagining different encounters with him. She is eager to be with him. At some point, she begins dreaming (although, it's unclear where the dream begins and ends); and her anxieties surface. In her dream, she rushes through the city to find her lover.

Some scholars believe that this passage is an analogy describing Israel's feelings of abandonment from Yahweh. Waking from sleep, Israel believes that God is gone. Israel searches for God, but to no avail. The sentinels may refer to prophets who spoke to Israel. Israel, however, passes by and doesn't listen to them. When Israel least expects it, Israel finds that Yahweh has been with them the whole time. When Israel finds God, they bring God back to the Temple.

Trailblazers

- **The Bride (the Shulammite)**
- **The Bridegroom (the Beloved)**

Nightmare gives way to fantasy as the girl dreams of her wedding day, beginning in verse 6. Her lover is described as a king. The image of Solomon's coming out of the wilderness could be compared with Israel's returning after the forty years in the wilderness.

- Have you ever felt as though someone you loved was missing? How did that make you feel?

② NOW READ SONG OF SOLOMON 3.

Switchback

Do you remember as a little kid being afraid when you were all by yourself in the house or when you got separated from your family at the mall? You probably got a knot in your stomach, wondering where your parents were. Maybe your heart started to race as you scanned the crowded stores for your older sibling. Relief set in quickly as you found your loved one and realized that you had not been abandoned.

This is another way of describing Israel's quest for God that is described in this poem. When the feeling of abandonment sets in, panic grows. The search for love becomes greater than we could ever have imagined. Israel often "fell asleep." In Israel's lack of faith, Israel believed that God had gone away. Israel searched frantically for Yahweh, only to discover that God was nearby all along.

How many times in our lives do we feel that God has left us? We begin seeking other ways to feel secure, but nothing satisfies. Know that God is always with you; and according to the Scriptures, God will never leave you or forsake you.

• Have you ever felt that God had left you all alone? What did you do?

• What assurance do we have that God will never leave us or forsake us?

Road Signs

- **sentinels** (3:3): These are guards or people keeping watch over or protecting people or property.
- **litter** (3:7): This is a curtained couch on poles. Usually two or more men hold the poles to carry the litter, which usually has only a single passenger
- **palanquin** (3:9): This is a covered litter that is carried on poles on the shoulders of four or more men.

 ### Prayer

Faithful Lord, keep me close to your heart and remind me that you are always with me, especially in times of doubt and uncertainty. Amen.

In the Eye of the Beholder
Song of Solomon 4

 Scouting the Terrain

The bridegroom uses some interesting descriptions to praise the woman's beauty. Imagine if you had overheard one of your friends tell his girlfriend that her hair was like a flock of goats or that her teeth were like freshly shorn female sheep! For the writer of the poem, however, these descriptions were quite flattering for his lover. In fact, in verse 7 he asserts that she has no flaw in her physical beauty.

The man's idyllic garden is sealed (for him), referring to the woman's virginity. The metaphor of the locked garden and all that it possesses is an allusion to sexual intimacy. As the chapter concludes, the woman invites the man into her garden. He accepts the invitation. Note the difference in pronoun usage in verse 16: first, the bride says, "my" garden. A few lines later, she says, "his" garden.

Trailblazers

- **The Bride (the Shulammite)**
- **The Bridegroom (the Beloved)**

• What do you learn from the Song of Solomon about God's plan and purpose for sexual relationships?

• How do you feel about the intimate details of the couple's sexual intimacy being included in the Bible? Does it make you uncomfortable? Why, or why not?

 NOW READ SONG OF SOLOMON 4.

③ Switchback

We live in a society that prizes physical beauty. We can't turn on the TV without being bombarded by dozens of ads that tell us that we need to look a certain way. In our culture, some people say things like, "She's (He's) not that good looking; love must be blind." The truth is that love *is* blind. It's not that love doesn't see physical differences; but that when love is real and genuine, physical beauty isn't defined by a standard. Beauty is defined by the heart of the one who adores the other. This is how God loves us. Despite our apparent differences, God loves us. It doesn't matter what flaws you think you have or the standards you set for yourself that you fail to meet. God sees you as beautiful.

• Have you ever felt that you were unattractive? What made you feel that way?

> **Road Signs**
> • **Gilead** (4:1): This region of ancient Palestine was east of the Jordan River in what is now just northwest of present-day Jordan.
> • **buckler** (4:4): This was a small, round shield that was worn on the arm during a battle.
> • **calamus** (4:14): This is an aromatic stem of the sweet flag (a perennial herb), which produces an oil used in perfumes.

• How important do you think physical attraction is to a relationship?

④ Prayer

Beautiful God, help me see myself and others through your eyes. Amen.

Song of Solomon

123

You Snooze . . .
Song of Solomon 5–6

 Scouting the Terrain

Once again, we find the bride searching for her lover in the nighttime. This time, the woman is awakened by her lover's knock on her door. He speaks to her in the early hours of the morning, telling her that the wet night air is a good reason for her to let him in the house. In verse 3, she tells him that she's already turned in for the night (she's in her PJs and her feet are clean). Her decline is merely a tease, though. When the man sticks his hand through the opening of the door, she longs for him. She goes to the door, ready to meet him; however, she finds that he is already gone. Unfortunately, she took too long. She heads out into the night after him. Notice the similarity to chapter 3. This time, however, when the sentinels find her, they beat her and strip her of her cloak. In the end, she is left longing for her lover.

Trailblazers

- **The Bride (the Shulammite)**
- **The Bridegroom (the Beloved)**
- **The Friends (the daughters of Jerusalem)**

She appeals to the daughters of Jerusalem to convey her longing for her lover, should they find him. The daughters of Jerusalem want to know what's so special about this guy. The bride then rattles off a detailed description of his physical attributes. This peaks their interest, and they offer to help search for him. Not so fast! The bride quickly points out that her bridegroom is not really lost. No, he's in his "garden," enjoying its delights. He is a faithful, monogamous lover.

- Why would the book use sexual imagery to demonstrate the intimacy between God and Israel?

- Do you think that this technique is effective or distracting?

WEEK 12

DAY 4

2.
NOW READ
SONG OF SOLOMON 5–6.